P9-DWC-070

CULTURAL ORIENTATIONS GUIDE

The Roadmap to Cultural Competence

FIFTH EDITION

Joerg Schmitz

Princeton Training Press
a TMC Company
Princeton, New Jersey USA

Cultural Orientations Guide

Published by:
PRINCETON TRAINING PRESS
Princeton, New Jersey

a TMC Company
600 Alexander Road
Princeton, New Jersey 08540-6011 USA

Tel: 609-951-0525
Fax: 609-951-0395
Web: www.tmcorp.com
E-mail: info@tmcorp.com

Editor-in-Chief: Tim Walker
Cover Design/Illustrations: Miguel Roman
Layout: Eric Charbonneau

©2006 TRAINING MANAGEMENT CORPORATION

Cultural Orientations Guide, Fifth Edition

All rights reserved. No part of this publication may be reproduced, stored in a retrieval system, or transmitted, in any form or by any means, electronic, mechanical, photocopying, recording or otherwise, without the prior written permission of the publisher.

Printed in the United States of America

ISBN: 1-882390-36-9

The Cultural Orientations Model™, COM™, and Cultural Orientations Indicator®, COI® are all trademarks of Training Management Corporation, Registration: 75-652669, 75-652654 and 75-6526710

Table of Contents

Preface...v

Part 1: Cultural Competence....................1

Part 2: Appreciating the Impact of Culture...9

Part 3: Cultural Due Diligence...................19

Part 4: Style Switching...........................109

Part 5: Cultural Dialogue and Cultural
         Mentoring..................................127

Part 6: Cultural Competence at Work.......149

Appendix A...165
Guide to Common Culture-Based
Challenges

Appendix B...169
Definition of Terms

Appendix C...173
Recommended Resources

Appendix D...179
Bibliography

Footnotes..181

About the Author..................................183

Cultural Orientations Guide

Preface

Culture plays an increasingly important role in the consciousness of individuals, organizations and entire societies. The mounting ethnic and religious tensions, "multi-culturalization" of our societies, and the international competition for human and natural resources cast a new light on the importance of culture. Cultural competence, in turn, enables the adaptability and flexibility needed to respond to the rapidly changing global context.

The fifth edition of the Cultural Orientations Guide (COG) is even more focused on the four skills that define cultural competence. This edition is intended to be a practical guide and development resource, providing specific reflection exercises and scenarios to guide the process of skill building. Together with the Cultural Orientations Indicator®, the COG is used at Harvard, MIT, UCLA, Columbia, Thunderbird, INSEAD/ CEDEP and the Center for Creative Leadership. Organizations such as Air Products and Chemicals, American Express, ArvinMeritor, BASF, BP, DaimlerChrysler, IBM, Novartis, Infosys, Kraft, Mastercard International, Merck, Procter & Gamble, Schering AG, Solvay Pharmaceuticals, Young & Rubicam Brands, and many others are actively using this approach and its related tools (including the Cultural Navigator™) to embed cultural competence into the fabric of their organizations.

I would like to thank our clients who have provided their feedback, thoughts and ideas; particularly Nancy Curl of IBM, Becky Bechtel of Air Products, Cindy Zimmerer and Bill Manfredi of Young and Rubicam, Leticia Knowles of American Express and Andreas Bauer of DaimlerChrysler. I am equally grateful to my friends and colleagues at TMC: Danielle and Tim Walker, David Lange, Kristen English, Pierre DeGroot, Claire-Marie Barth, Eric Charbonneau, Andrew Trksak, Miguel Roman, Susan Scherer, Shaun College, Angela Yen, Alina Enggist, Sonia Rodriguez and Suzanna Rosenberg, who all have contributed to this Guide.

My deepest gratitude and appreciation goes to my wife Latha and my daughter Christina, to whom this Guide is dedicated.

Joerg Schmitz
Princeton, 1 September 2006

Culture will be, as it always has been, of critical importance in deciding the relative fortunes of the major world economies. Those institutions and organizations that recognize and articulate this fact will have the lead on those that neglect it.

Culture Wars
by John Viney

PART 1

Cultural Competence

John Viney's quote, as poignant as it is, forgets to mention that recognizing and articulating the importance of culture is, in itself, insufficient. Only action guided by the conscious awareness of culture's critical importance will yield the desired success.

Cultural competence is about such action. It is *the ability to reduce the risks and maximize the opportunities inherent in cultural differences and similarities, as well as culture-based performance and success factors.* In complex, diverse global organizations and their international marketplace, this ability is increasingly important. It enables responsiveness, speed and adaptability. It is the *bonding agent* in the dichotomy between global and local operations, and the underpinning for innovation, growth, speed, high-performance, and adaptability.

The Five Levels of Cultural Competence

Cultural competence can be applied at the same levels at which culture operates; namely (1) national/societal (also market), (2) organization, (3) business unit/functional, (4) team/group and (5) individual/ interpersonal.

1. At the **national/societal level**, cultural competence describes the ability to constructively adapt to changing social, political, economic, environmental, and/or demographic conditions. Cultural competence at this level is a key aspect to ensuring the prosperity, viability and even survival of a given social group. This is arguably the most difficult level of culture and the responsibility of leaders within a given nation, society and/or social group.

2. At an **organization level**, cultural competence enables the organization to strategically adapt and develop its culture to the changing performance and talent requirements of their respective sphere of influence/marketplace. For most organizations (profit or non-profit, governmental or private) this sphere of influence/marketplace is increasingly marked by internationalization or globalization.

   Cultural competence at this level encompasses the effective integration of differing organization cultures, engaging globally diverse talent, and optimizing organization-wide learning, innovation, speed and growth. It is the responsibility of organizational leaders and a critical aspect in their development.

3. At a **business unit/functional level**, cultural competence enables: (a) the bridging of cultural gaps; (b) the importing, exchanging and creation of knowledge; (c) the negotiation of compatible business processes and practices; and (d) the development of synergies across functions, including customers and suppliers.

   Cultural differences at this level tend to be very pronounced. However, the increasing reliance on cross-functional teamwork and collaboration requires a widespread and embedded ability to reduce the cultural risk factors to optimal performance. This is the responsibility of everybody in cross-functional teams or work groups and an important domain for functional leaders.

4. At a **team/group level,** cultural competence enables a team or work group to: (a) effectively integrate new talent, (b) leverage knowledge and skill resources, (c) engage its stakeholders (including customers and/or clients), (d) develop and sustain effective and inclusive operating principles and practices, and (e) adapt to change.

The increasing diversity of the workforce, together with the specific challenges faced by global teams (i.e., transcending language, time zones, communication, as well as cultural differences) highlights cultural competence at this level. It is the responsibility of all members of diverse and global teams, but particularly their respective leaders.

5. At the **individual/interpersonal level,** cultural competence enables individual employees, managers, and leaders to operate effectively in the midst of ambiguity, uncertainty, and complexity of a culturally diverse employee-, customer-, and supplier base (as well as geographically dispersed matrix relationships). In such work contexts, it is particularly the ability to influence, persuade and build trust that enables individual effectiveness. Where these are requirements for success; insight into the culture-based expectations and practices of counterparts, co-workers, clients, etc., is key.

Cultural competence has always played such a critical role, but never before has it emerged so consciously as in the complex, globally interconnected, dynamic world of the 21st century. Never before has the need to consciously focus on the elements of cultural competence, and purposefully apply them, been so important or relevant.

The Elements of Cultural Competence

Cultural competence is the outcome of a continuous learning process. The more an individual engages in this learning process, the greater the cultural competence they exhibit.

Figure 1. – Key Skills

Open Attitude	Receptive to cross-cultural learning and maintains an open and productive attitude toward difference. Continuously challenges assumptions about other cultures. Avoids quick judgments. Tolerates ambiguity and complexity in cross-cultural social situations. Remains patient with others. Continuously pursues learning about other cultures.
Self-Awareness	Is aware of and knowledgeable about one's own cultural preferences. Can articulate one's own cultural values, beliefs, attitudes and how they are reflected in behavior. Can identify how differences between one's own culture and another's culture could lead to misunderstandings. Is aware of how interaction with another culture makes one uncomfortable. Can identify ways to adapt that will support cross-cultural interactions.
Other-Awareness	Recognizes the cultural values, attitudes, beliefs and behaviors of others in order to develop new cross-cultural business skills. Correctly identifies the cultural preferences of one's counterparts and how they are expressed in their behavior. Observes and articulates areas of shared cultural perspectives to find common ground. Gauges one's counterpart's willingness to learning about one's own cultural preferences. Identifies ways to build stronger cross-cultural relationships.
Cultural Knowledge	Has acquired, or can acquire as necessary, a comprehensive knowledge of other specific social and business cultures. Correctly identifies the general knowledge needed about a culture. Gathers specific business or industry knowledge to conduct business in this context. Studies how the culture's outlook on life has been shaped by history. Can identify how in this culture conflict is resolved, decisions are made, problems are solved, people are motivated, performance is rewarded, relationships are established and maintained, negotiations are conducted, people

	are led. Knows where to get necessary information and builds networks of contacts who can offer insight into other cultures.
Cultural Skills	Have the necessary skills to work effectively across cultures in many different business contexts. Can translate cultural awareness and knowledge into skills. Improves one's own ability to work in multicultural situations. Continues to refine and improve one's skills. Adapts one's own business practices or management skills appropriately to particular cultures and situations. Negotiations are conducted and people are led. Knows where to get necessary information and builds networks of contacts who can offer insight into other cultures.

Cultural Skills

Four specific skills are associated with cultural competence. They can be observed in the behaviors of individuals, the processes of teams, and the systems and procedures of organizations:

1. **Cultural Due Diligence** is *the practice to assess and prepare for the possible impact of culture.* Cultural Due Diligence requires a non-judgmental understanding of cultural differences and a well developed self-awareness.

2. **Style-Switching** is *the ability to use a different behavioral approach to accomplish one's goals.* Style-Switching can be a difficult skill to develop and sustain. It requires a broad and flexible behavioral repertoire that is built on the basis of focused reflection on one's own culture-based values, beliefs, preferences, and behaviors.

3. **Cultural Dialogue** is *the ability to explore cultural differences and negotiate mutual adaptations through conversation.* Cultural Dialogue requires the application of a carefully crafted conversational process.

4. **Cultural Mentoring** is *the ability to help others with cultural adaptation and integration.* Cultural Mentoring requires applying one's own awareness, knowledge and insight for the benefit of another individual or group.

The importance and relevance of cultural competence and the commitment to developing its hallmark skills are based on appreciating the impact of culture on interactions and ventures at every level.

As a comprehensive guide for developing cultural competence, this book starts with this pre-requisite and then focuses on each skill separately. Examples and case studies are chosen to illustrate key aspects or as an opportunity to practice. The final section, *Cultural Competence at Work,* consists of a collection of cases and scenarios that allow a comprehensive practice of all cultural skills. They are chosen to represent all levels at which culture operates.

Key Learning Points: Introduction

o Cultural Competence is *the ability to reduce the risks and maximize the opportunities inherent in cultural differences and similarities, as well as culture-based performance and success factors.*

o In complex, diverse global organizations and their international marketplace, this ability is increasingly important as it enables responsiveness, speed and adaptability.

o Cultural Competence can be applied at the same levels at which culture operates, namely (1) national/societal (also market), (2) organization, (3) business unit/functional, (4) team/group and (5) individual/ interpersonal.

o The continuous learning process that characterizes Cultural Competence leads to four specific skills, namely (a) cultural due diligence, (b) style-switching, (c) cultural dialogue, and (d) cultural mentoring.

*In culture, we must imagine a
great arc on which are ranged
the possible interests provided
either by the human age-cycle
or by environment, or by man's
various activities. ... Every
human society everywhere has
made a selection in its cultural
institutions. Each from the
point of view of another ignores
fundamentals and exploits
irrelevancies.*

*Patterns of Culture
by Ruth Benedict*

PART 2

Appreciating the Impact of Culture

Successfully building cultural competence rests on understanding culture and appreciating how profoundly our values, attitudes and behaviors are affected by it. The goal of this section is to define and explore the concept of culture and introduce a framework for understanding the way it operates as either a risk or success factor in our actions and interactions.

Understanding Culture

Culture is a complex phenomenon and a difficult concept to understand and manage[1]. It encompasses such tangible elements as language, food, dress, religion, customs and artifacts as well as intangible elements, some of which are a social group's values, beliefs and assumptions along with the emotions with which these are invested. The strong emotional component of culture seems often overlooked in many models and literature on culture; however, it is critical to any appreciation of culture and its impact.

9

It is precisely the emotional rootedness of behavior that explains why culture change is so intricate, difficult and often unpredictable; or why culture and ethnicity are the seeming battlegrounds in the globally interconnected 21st century. A meaningful definition and framework of culture needs to account for this strong emotional component.

Culture can be defined as *the complex pattern of ideas, emotions, and observable manifestations (behaviors and/or symbols) that tend to be expected, reinforced and rewarded by and within a particular group.* How this definition helps understand and appreciate the impact of culture is illustrated as follows:

In many Western cultures, individual assertiveness is considered an asset and generally expected, reinforced and rewarded. For most of these cultures, assertiveness is positively evaluated as an indication of competence and linked to feelings of admiration, trust, and pride.

Behavioral identifiers of assertiveness in such cultures include eye contact, a firm handshake, a strong and definite tone of voice, the absence of qualifiers (such as "maybe," "perhaps," "probably," etc.) and other indicators of "tentativeness" from a speaker's words, as well as a higher frequency of control elements in language (e.g., questions and declarative statements).

Assertiveness is also linked to and expected in particular social situations. In the U.S., individual assertiveness is a success factor in most job interviews. The meaning of the behaviors associated with good interviewing is specific to the U.S. cultural milieu; it is not universal.

Cultural gaps result when individuals interact with different expectations and assumptions on behavioral patterns and their meaning.

In job interviews, for example, the attribute of assertiveness is greatly

Culture: (full definition) *the complex pattern of ideas, emotions, and observable manifestations (behaviors and/or symbols) that tend to be expected, reinforced and rewarded by and within a particular group.*

(short definition) *what is expected, reinforced and rewarded within a particular social group.*

valued in a U.S. cultural context, but often conflicts with values and behaviors that are expected, reinforced and rewarded in many European and Asian contexts. A European job applicant may greet the interviewer with a strong handshake and may make eye contact, but his/her frequent use of qualifiers, tentativeness and a lower tone of voice may not communicate the level of confidence the U.S. interviewer requires for a favorable evaluation.

An interviewer who does not understand that the threshold for evaluating assertiveness as overbearing, arrogant and impolite is lower in many European contexts and can result in overlooking and dismissing valuable talent.

An Asian job applicant's handshake may not apply sufficient pressure to create the impression of assertiveness as evaluated in the U.S., and he/she may deem it inappropriate to make eye contact or may use language that is relatively tentative. Furthermore, both the European and Asian applicants may not associate the context of a job interview with the expectation of demonstrating a high level of individual assertiveness.

The above example illustrates the profound effect culture has on critical business situations. It shows the interdependence of the levels at which culture occurs (i.e., societal/market, organization, functional, team and individual).

Although culture is an attribute of social groups, it manifests itself in the interaction between individuals, and so it is at the level of interactions that we can identify culture. Consequently, we need to sharpen our awareness of how the values, behaviors and views of our counterparts reflect the cultural orientations prevalent in the social environments that have shaped his/her person. And through interaction we will discover our own cultural values, behaviors and perspectives.

At each level of culture, the role of the individual in cultural processes differs significantly: At the societal/national, organization and functional level the individual uniquely reflects and reproduces cultural patterns (unless he/she occupies a key leadership position). At the team and the interpersonal level, the individual has more influence on cultural processes. Whether we want to understand cultural processes or change them, it is the individual, interpersonal level at which we need to start.

The cornerstone of developing cultural competence is therefore an individual journey of learning, development and growth.

A Framework for Understanding the Impact of Culture

The full impact and importance of culture only becomes evident when we experience a culture gap. However, most people think of a culture gap as a clash of different behaviors, such as extending one's hand when the other person bows, or announcing a decision when everyone else in the meeting expects the decision to be made by consensus.

These are *behavioral expressions* of a culture gap, but there are at least two other kinds of culture gaps that (a) are not easily detectable, (b) are likely more prevalent than behavioral ones, and (c) may carry more risk when <u>not</u> considered or addressed. These are:

Cognitive Gap: An individual is fully cognizant of a fundamental difference between expectations and actions. For example, a person who perceives time as fluid may report to a supervisor who expects fixed-time behavior. However, a fluid time-oriented person, cognizant of such a gap, may continue to engage in various activities, such as setting their watches early or habitually arriving early for appointments to meet the other's expectations. The fluid-time-oriented person experiences this **culture gap** cognitively; he/she is completely aware of the **social distance** created by two very different orientations to time.

> **Social distance** is the dissonance or alienation experienced when a behavior or event does not meet one's expectations.

Emotional Gap: An individual experiences strong emotions, mostly negative ones, as a result of differing cultural orientations. These emotions can be mild, causing low levels of discomfort, uneasiness or impatience; or they can be strong, resulting in overt or covert anger and aggression. For example, the fixed-time-oriented individual may get annoyed and frustrated and/or experience other strong emotions as a reaction to a fluid-time-oriented individual. The emotional reactions engendered by this **culture gap** may or may not be acted on or even recognized. In other words, the **social distance** may be experienced emotionally but not manifest itself behaviorally or even cognitively.

All three manifestations of a culture gap (behavioral[2], cognitive, and emotional) and the social distance each engenders cause stress, tension and both internal and external conflict. This stress, tension and conflict need to be properly managed in order to increase individual effectiveness in a multicultural context.

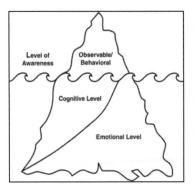

The three ways that one experiences cultural variation can be illustrated by the metaphor of the iceberg.

While behavioral difference is "on the surface" and therefore readily noticeable, emotional and cognitive differences lie beneath the surface and may remain largely out of awareness. The foundation upon which cultural competence rests is comprised of a sound understanding of the various cultural orientations, their impact on interactions and their identifying behavioral expressions.

The general framework for understanding how culture operates and how cultural gaps are experienced distinguishes between the behavioral, cognitive (beliefs) and emotional aspects.

The following provides a specific example for applying this framework for understanding specific cultural differences and their effect on a business venture. The case of Monsanto's introduction of Genetically Modified Foods (GMF) to the European market is a good example.

Framework	Monsanto	European Market
Behavioral Level ➤	Enthusiastic product launch	Broad based rejection
Cognitive (Belief) Level ➤	• More efficient • Ecologically better • Safer & reduced erosion • Less fuel intensive • New = better • Farmers will love it • Shareholders will love it • Customers & shareholders are who matter	• Tampering with genetics is dangerous • New is not better • Unproven, untested products with wide exposure to people • Food is culture – don't alter it • We need to be involved • Consumers were not considered • American multinational's presumptuous approach
Emotional Level ➤	Optimistic enthusiasm	Fear

As the above example illustrates; distinguishing between behavioral, cognitive, and emotional levels provides a succinct and powerful way to comprehensively understand cultural differences and their impact. This framework allows a differentiated understanding instrumental to cultural competence and the associated skills.

Practice Scenarios

Each of the following scenarios is an example of the impact of culture. For each, identify the link between the behavioral, cognitive (belief) and emotional levels of culture.

1. **A Simple Change in Schedule**
   Mr. Zheng, a Chinese manager with ample experience, knowledge and connections to key government, municipal and business officials, has a good rapport with Mr. Johnson, his contact from the U.K. parent organization that is engaged in a joint venture in China. When Mr. Johnson asked Mr. Zheng to postpone their meeting by months, he replied, "I don't think it's a good idea. It would be better to go ahead with the meeting." Mr. Johnson started probing for reasons, but Mr. Zheng appeared unwilling to share information. The more Mr. Johnson probed the more defensive, closed and vague Mr. Zheng became.

   On Mr. Johnson's insistence, the meeting was postponed. When the meeting finally took place, Mr. Johnson was upset that, against the previous commitment, the Chinese company sent only lower-level representatives unprepared to move the project along.

2. **The Performance Management System**
   Lisa Knowles, new VP in the Geddy Global Business Unit (a recent acquisition by Liggert) is running her first annual performance rating session for all Marketing Directors (MDs) and Brand Managers (BMs). She appointed one of her GMs to collaborate with the HR Manager to plan and lead the session.

   The contribution forms were all submitted, but only the "what" for results is fully complete. Most forms are only partially filled in or blank for the "how." The Geddy managers only want to review the results of performance measures. They are not interested in discussing how people got the results, only what they delivered.

   It's the break in the session, they are way behind, and Ms. Knowles feels very frustrated and uncomfortable with how this is going. She keeps asking for more information on how the MDs and BMs are building the organization. In response, the GMs either question why it matters or they are silent. She has conducted many ratings sessions during her career at Liggert and it's never been so difficult.

3. **The Unexpected Resignation**
   Mrs. Tamatsukuri, a Japanese employee of a U.S. company in Tokyo, is experiencing a problem. Frequently, Mr. Snyder, her boss and an expatriate from the United States, gives her what she sees as unrealistic timelines for completing her projects.

   She manages to complete her work on time, but only through great personal sacrifice including working late, coming into the office on weekends, and getting her colleagues to assist her. Her boss is very pleased. He often praises her in weekly staff meetings and asks for her opinion in front of others.

   When after several months Mrs. Tamatsukuri submits her resignation, citing family obligations as the official reason for leaving, Mr. Snyder is completely taken by surprise. Mrs. Tamatsukuri has, in reality, decided to seek employment with another company because of her guilt and shame for having been singled out by Mr. Snyder in front of peers. She also hopes she will be able to meet the demands of her new job without having to do so at such a high personal cost.

4. **Feedback**
   Mr. van Groet, a Dutch supervisor, is meeting with Mr. Al-Kathani, a Saudi Arabian, to provide feedback on his performance at work. "As you know, you're strong in most areas. However, there are a couple of areas where you could improve. One is in report writing, which isn't easy for you, is it?" Mr. Al-Kathani looks down and simply says, "I see." Mr. van Groet continues, "Otherwise, there are no serious problems and, in general, you are doing a fine job." Mr. Al-Kathani, his glance still lowered, responds: "I'm very sorry to disappoint you, sir."

5. **An Exciting Time**
   This is an exciting time. You are participating in the first truly European meeting of your newly restructured, now regional,

organization. Unfortunately, the synergies that you hoped would develop are not evident anywhere.

The Swiss-German VP of your organization provides an initial presentation. With a very heavy accent and long-winded sentences, he commences with a very detailed background on the history of the company before the restructuring. He reviews the core principles upon which the organization has relied while facing many economic and social challenges throughout its history. Upon this review, he explains the logic of the reorganization and discusses the implications for meeting the project demands of the marketplace over the next decade.

You notice that most of the audience has disengaged halfway through the first part of the presentation. Representatives from the U.K. and the Netherlands are getting particularly restless. Others are straining simply to understand the presentation. Some of the Southern representatives seem to be falling asleep.

To validate the linkages between the levels of culture in each scenario, open the URL below and click on the scenario: https://bookstore.culturalnavigator.com/cog.

Key Learning Points: Appreciating the Impact of Culture

o Our values, attitudes and behaviors are profoundly affected by culture.

o Culture is *the complex pattern of ideas, emotions, and observable manifestations (behaviors and/or symbols) that tend to be expected, reinforced and rewarded by and within a particular group.*

o The strong emotional component of culture is often overlooked in many models and literature on culture, but emphasized by the Cultural Orientations Approach.

o Cultural gaps often produce an experience of social distance at the behavioral, cognitive (belief), and/or emotional level.

In a multicultural environment, whatever you have learned is unreliable at best.

It is riskier to assume similarity and later find out that significant differences exist, than to assume differences until similarity is proven.

Adapted from Nancy Adler

PART 3

Cultural Due Diligence

This section introduces the first of the four skills associated with cultural competence: Cultural Due Diligence. It is *the practice to assess and prepare for the possible impact of culture*. This skill relies on a non-judgmental understanding of cultural differences and a well developed self-awareness. This section introduces:

> ➢ the Cultural Orientations Model™ as a non-judgmental reference to the key dimensions across which cultures differ,
> ➢ the Cultural Orientations Indicator® as a key tool for developing cultural self-awareness, and
> ➢ specific recommendations for using these to assess and prepare for the possible impact of culture.

Cultural Due Diligence is a form of risk assessment. Basically, it consists of the following steps:

(1) investigating and determining the cultural backgrounds and orientations of one's colleagues, counterparts, partners, clients, etc.;

(2) evaluating potential or actual cultural gaps;

(3) identifying the potential or actual impact of these gaps on one's objectives (both negative and positive); and

(4) developing a strategy for minimizing any resulting negative effects.

Cultural Due Diligence is best exercised in preparation for management interactions and business engagements (partnership projects, etc.). It involves a process, one strives to understand the history, backgrounds and experiences that have shaped the perspective, outlook and value system of specific individuals and/or groups with whom you are communicating and interacting.

To perform Cultural Due Diligence, one has to make inferences and form hypotheses from a variety of sources, including observation and interviewing. Both activities should be based on an awareness of key dimensions of culture and their general variability.

The Cultural Orientations Model™ is a useful framework for building this awareness. It organizes the wide spectrum of variability in values and norms among human groups, cultural environments and social situations. Most importantly, it provides a shared, non-judgmental vocabulary for assessing challenges related to culture.

The Cultural Orientations Model™

This model summarizes research-based concepts[3] and consists of 10 cultural dimensions, with 17 cultural continua and 36 orientations.

The 10 Dimensions of Culture:

Environment	How individuals view and relate to the people, objects and issues in their sphere of influence.
Time	How individuals perceive the nature of time and its use.
Action	How individuals conceptualize actions and interactions.
Communication	How individuals express themselves.
Space	How individuals demarcate their physical and psychological space.
Power	How individuals view differential power relationships.
Individualism	How individuals define their identity.
Competitiveness	How individuals are motivated.
Structure	How individuals approach change, risk, ambiguity and uncertainty.
Thinking	How individuals conceptualize.

Cultural Continuum

A cultural continuum is a spectrum between opposing orientations within a cultural dimension. Figure 2 illustrates this idea.

Dimension: Communication

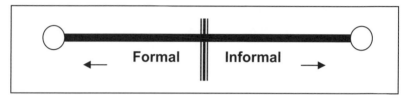

Figure 2: Cultural Continuum

Cultural Orientations

Cultural orientations define each side of the Cultural Continuum. A cultural orientation is a particular culture-based value which is (a) more or less favored, expected or desired by the members of a given social group, or (b) expected, reinforced and rewarded in a given social situation or environment.

In Figure 2 above, the cultural orientation is either *formal* or *informal*. If a given social group were indicated as *informal,* we could assume that this group and the majority of its members will:

➢ exhibit more informal behavior patterns,

➢ experience more discomfort with formal behaviors, and

➢ generally strive to reduce formal situations.

An informal orientation would *NOT* indicate the absence of formality, but a relative reduction and dislike of formality as compared to other groups. In fact, much like dominant or recessive genes, cultural orientations may describe dominant or recessive characteristics of groups. The relationship between cultural orientations may not be as linear as Figure 2 suggests. It may be more useful to think of their relationship of interdependence and dynamic counterbalance, much like the relationship between Ying and Yang (see Figure 3).

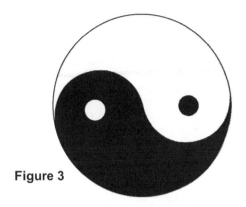

Figure 3

Most cultural orientations exist within any given group. When compared between groups, each differentially favors, and/or associates them with different situations and contexts. In fact, each social group is guided by such a *situational code*[4] providing its members through the multitude of social interactions and organizational challenges.

Cultural Orientations Model™: Quickview

This model provides a concise non-judgmental vocabulary to refer to cultural gaps and similarities among individuals and groups.

ENVIRONMENT

Social environments can be categorized according to whether they view and relate to people, objects and issues from the orientation of *control, harmony* or *constraint.* A *control* orientation is indicated by a strong attitude that the environment can and should be changed and molded to fit one's needs. *Harmony* is indicated by a need to build consensus and balance all interests. A *constraint* orientation is indicated by a need to act within clearly defined parameters set by external forces. A key question is: How do the actions, behaviors, business practices and processes reflect either a *control, harmony* or *constraint* attitude?

TIME

Social environments differ in how time is perceived and used. A *single-focus* orientation is indicated by concentrating on one task at a time, while a *multi-focus* orientation in indicated by attending to multiple tasks and/or relationships simultaneously. Key questions to ask: How are tasks/relationships handled? What are the implicit norms and values that guide behavior?

A *fixed* orientation is indicated by primarily focusing on an exact measurement of time. A *fluid* orientation is indicated by having a secondary focus on the exact measurement of time. Key questions to ask: How much attention is placed on the exact measurement of time? What is the implicitly acceptable variance from a stated time or deadline?

A *past* orientation is indicated by placing a high value on pre-established processes and procedures. A *present* orientation is indicated by placing a focus on short-term and quick results. A *future* orientation is indicated by placing a focus on long-term results. A key question to ask: Are decisions guided by the past, present or future orientation?

ACTION

Social environments can be distinguished by the way they approach actions and interactions. An emphasis on relationship, reflection and analysis indicates a *being* orientation. A focus on task and action indicates a *doing* orientation. Key questions to ask: How is the relationship between action and reflection structured? Where is the emphasis? How much value is placed on building and maintaining a relationship over accomplishing tasks and action items?

COMMUNICATION

Social environments can be distinguished by the value orientations that govern how individuals express themselves. An emphasis on implicit communication and reliance on non-verbal cues indicates a *high-context* orientation. A *low-context* orientation is indicated by a strong value on explicit communication. Key questions are: How are meaning and information related? How readily do individuals assume hidden meanings in messages?

A *direct* orientation is indicated by a perceived value of conflict and a preference for its direct and explicit handling. An *indirect* orientation is associated with the use of implicit modes and/or third parties in conflict situations and tends to be associated with the value of conflict avoidance. Key questions are: What is the value of conflict? What are the expectations for handling conflict?

Emphasizing and valuing displays of emotion and/or eloquent uses of language indicate an *expressive* orientation. An *instrumental* orientation is indicated by valuing factual, detached and dispassionate interactions and communication styles. A key question is: How is the degree of instrumental or expressive behaviors linked to the notions of professionalism and professional behavior?

An emphasis on protocol, customs and/or set processes indicates a *formal* orientation. An emphasis on dispensing with ceremony and protocol indicates an *informal* orientation. Key questions are: What is the value placed on protocol, customs and set processes? How are they linked to behaviors and practices?

SPACE
Cultures can be categorized according to the distinctions they make between *public* and *private* spaces. This includes distances between individuals and the organization of work space, as well as how information is shared. It is often useful to think about cultural space in terms of two questions: How much space do people want around them personally or at work? How does this affect the sharing of information?

POWER
Social environments can be categorized by the way they structure power relationships. A *hierarchy* orientation is indicated by having a high degree of acceptability of different power relationships and social stratification. An *equality* orientation is indicated by showing little tolerance for differential power relationships and a minimization of social stratification. Key questions are: How acceptable are hierarchal relationships? How does the value on equality or hierarchy guide behavior, business practices and processes?

INDIVIDUALISM
Social environments can be distinguished by the ways in which individuals define their identity. An emphasis on independence and a focus on the individual indicate an *individualistic* orientation. An emphasis on affiliation and subordination of individual interests to that of the group, company or organization indicates a *collectivistic* orientation. Key questions are: Do individuals identify themselves more through membership of a group or as individual contributors? What expectations does the group, company or organization have on an individual's behavior?
A *universalistic* orientation is indicated by exhibiting a value of standards, processes, procedures, rules and laws to govern situations equally. A *particularistic* orientation is indicated by placing values on uniqueness, difference and situational context in determining the way in which issues are handled. A key question: What is the implicit understanding of and perceived need to comply with rules, laws, processes and procedures?

COMPETITIVENESS

Social environments can be categorized by how people are motivated. An emphasis on personal achievements, individual assertiveness and success indicate a **competitive** orientation. Valuing quality of life, interdependence and relationships indicate a **cooperative** orientation. A social group may be internally cooperative and externally competitive, or vice-versa. Key questions are: What values motivate individuals, the group or organization? How do behaviors, decisions and processes reflect this value?

STRUCTURE

Social environments can be distinguished by their tolerance of ambiguity and uncertainty. Environments that value adherence to rules, regulations and procedures are considered **order** oriented and prefer predictability and minimization of risk. Environments that value improvisation exhibit a **flexibility** orientation and tend to reward risk-taking, tolerate ambiguity and value innovation. Key questions are: What is the prevailing attitude towards ambiguity and uncertainty? How are these attitudes expressed in behavior, processes and practices?

THINKING

Social environments can be distinguished by the emphasis on and reinforcement of different approaches to thinking and conceptualizing. They can either expect, reinforce and reward a **deductive** approach (an emphasis on theory, principles, concepts and abstract logic) or an **inductive** approach (value reasoning based on experience, in particular incident and experimentation). They may also either emphasize a **linear** approach (analysis and segmentation of issues) or a **systemic** approach (synthesis, holism and the "big picture"). A key question is: How do people perceive the value of and relationship between (1) concepts and abstract thinking and (2) data and experience? How is that reflected in the way people argue and present information?

The Cultural Orientations Indicator®

To assess and prepare for the possible impact of culture, it is necessary yet insufficient to understand the spectrum of cultural variation. To truly assess potential culture gaps and associated risks, we need to understand our own cultural preferences and inclinations. The Cultural Orientations Indicator® is a self-assessment tool designed to provide these insights.

When reviewing your personal Cultural Orientations Indicator®, keep in mind that it:

- is descriptive rather than prescriptive, displaying in an organized format the preferences you selected on a self-report instrument.
- describes general preferences, not skills, abilities or particular behaviors.
- is restricted to work-related behaviors and situations.
- is subject to self-validation, as is any assessment instrument.

Activity

1. Explore each cultural continuum and its related orientations.

2. Identify specific interactions in your sphere of influence where gaps between the orientations are involved.

3. Assess the positive and negative consequences of these gaps.

The following pages summarize the implications for individuals for each cultural orientation recognized by the Cultural Orientations Model™. Please refer to the index on the next page to locate the specific descriptions.

Index

Dimension	Orientation	Page	Dimension	Orientation	Page
Environment	Control	30	Power	Hierarchy	74
	Harmony	32		Equality	77
	Constraint	34			
Time	Single-focus	36	Individual-ism	Individualistic	79
	Multi-focus	38		Collectivistic	82
	Fixed	40		Universalistic	84
	Fluid	42		Particularistic	86
	Past	44			
	Present	46			
	Future	48			
Action	Being	50	Competitive-ness	Competitive	88
	Doing	52		Cooperative	90
Communication	High-context	54	Structure	Order	92
	Low-context	56		Flexibility	94
	Direct	58			
	Indirect	60			
	Expressive	62			
	Instrumental	64			
	Formal	66			
	Informal	68			
Space	Private	70	Thinking	Deductive	96
	Public	72		Inductive	98
				Linear	100
				Systemic	102

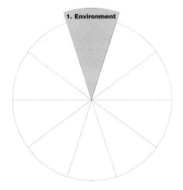

Dimension: Environment

How individuals view and relate to the people, objects and issues in their sphere of influence.

Orientation: Control

Social environments that tend to expect, reward and reinforce a **control** orientation emphasize that people can and should influence and change their environment to fit their needs.

Description

You are a strong believer in the saying: "Where there's a will, there's a way," and you believe that your destiny is primarily in your own hands. When you encounter problems, you immediately look for a solution. You approach the world with a natural sense of "empowerment." You view very few problems as insurmountable. You have a need for individual ownership of tasks and problems in your immediate environment.

You often assume that objects and people in your surroundings should conform to your preferred approach, methods and processes. You tend to be proactive, self-driven and assertive and find that you naturally take initiative. You want to take charge of situations and do not shy away from conflict and risk. You get frustrated with people who do not seem actively engaged in problem solving, do not share your sense of priorities or seem to lack initiative.

When this orientation is strong or very strong, you may:

- be perceived as aggressive and/or confrontational.
- assume that you will lead and direct in most situations.

- become easily annoyed, frustrated and impatient with those who do not share your orientation and attitude toward problem solving.
- tend to overestimate yourself and your ability to get things done.

Identifiers
People with this orientation frequently:

- are among the first ones in a group of equals to assume a leadership role.
- display a high degree of optimism when confronting a problem.
- trust in, value and emphasize pragmatic tools and techniques.
- advocate personal accountability and risk-taking.
- use declarative statements and closed (yes/no) questions with high frequency when speaking.
- display impatience with intangible and vague statements, assessments and evaluations.

Learning Objectives
Your learning challenges are to:

- approach new situations more carefully and slowly.
- develop patience.
- phase-in your initiatives and contributions incrementally.

Reflection

1. How do you experience this orientation?
2. In which situations do you tend to act on this orientation?
3. Which influences and experiences have shaped your preference?
4. How are the learning objectives relevant to you?

Dimension: Environment

Orientation: Harmony
Social environments that tend to expect, reward and reinforce a **harmony** orientation to the environment emphasize the importance of balance and harmony with external forces in one's surroundings.

Description
It is important for you to maintain a balanced relationship with your social, natural and physical environment. You adjust your style and approach to the expectations and conditions of your surroundings in order to bring about balance.

Decision making and consensus-building with all parties involved in an interaction are key values that drive your behavior in social as well as business environments. Establishing and maintaining positive relationships is of key importance to you. You tend to avoid conflict and direct confrontation. You value flexibility and diplomacy and expect the same of others. When proposing a new idea or making plans, you readily assume a compromise will be required. You dislike radical change and champion the careful contemplation and testing of innovative solutions.

When this orientation is strong or very strong, you may:

- be too conciliatory and appear weak to others.
- frequently avoid situations in which you are required to take a strong position.
- act as a facilitator when you are expected to provide clear direction.
- be afraid to make controversial decisions.
- shy away from assuming individual responsibility and accountability.

Identifiers
People with this orientation may be identified by:

- a frequent use of qualifiers and open-ended questions when speaking.
- very gradual self-disclosure as relationships become more firmly established.

- a high degree of (visual) distress in confrontational situations.
- a frequently expressed need to assume the role of facilitator and mediator.

Learning Objectives

Your learning challenges are to:

- articulate a position and opinion firmly without considering those of others.
- develop individual assertiveness skills.
- take risks when it would be advisable.
- decrease your resistance to change, at times.

Reflection

1. How do you experience this orientation?
2. In which situations do you tend to act on this orientation?
3. Which influences and experiences have shaped your preference?
4. How are the learning objectives relevant to you?

Dimension: Environment

Orientation: Constraint

Social environments that tend to expect, reward and reinforce a **constraint** orientation to the environment emphasize the primary importance of external forces and conditions as defining parameters in human activities.

Description

You feel that you must live and act within the given limits of your environment. You see the world as immutable and trust that, in the larger scheme of things, situations will generally work out. You see it as presumptuous, even naïve, to claim direct control over organizational and/or business environments.

You often experience problems or resistance to your ideas or goals as obstacles that cannot be overcome. You generally accept the *status quo* and adjust your own behavior and expectations to the limits as presented to you. You do not feel naturally "empowered" to alter those limits in any way.

Your approach to problems and situations is often reactive and risk-averse. You prefer to behave according to a model and/or clear instructions and guidelines. You expect superiors or people in power to make decisions on your behalf.

When this orientation is strong or very strong, you may:

- be extraordinarily careful and cautious when approaching an unfamiliar situation and/or task.
- require detailed instructions on a given project.
- need very clearly defined and delineated responsibilities and expectations.
- be perceived as obstructionist and inflexible by those who do not share your orientation.
- be insecure about taking charge in ambiguous and vaguely defined situations.

Identifiers
People with this orientation may be identified by:

- their frequent references to and caution with respect to problems, obstacles and risks.
- their frequent requests for clear instructions and patience.
- their use of passive and negative sentence structures.
- their references to pre-established procedures, processes and guidelines as binding and immutable.

Learning Objectives
Your learning challenges are to:

- think of obstacles as opportunities and challenges.
- engage in creative problem solving to reduce the frequency of negative statements or concerns.
- take care not to hamper organizational dynamism and flexibility.
- be proactive rather than reactive, when possible.

Reflection

1. How do you experience this orientation?
2. In which situations do you tend to act on this orientation?
3. Which influences and experiences have shaped your preference?
4. How are the learning objectives relevant to you?

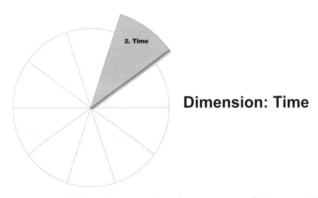

Dimension: Time

How individuals perceive the nature of time and its use.

Orientation: Single-Focus

Social environments that tend to expect, reward and reinforce a **single-focus** orientation to time and its use emphasize the importance of concentrating on one task at a time and demonstrate a precise commitment to schedules and timelines.

Description

You prefer to work on one thing at a time and break down work into a series of tasks, which you handle sequentially. You tend to have a high commitment to schedules, which you see as effective tools for ordering tasks. You are generally analytical in your approach to problem solving. You consider it impolite or unprofessional to talk to several people simultaneously about different things.

When this orientation is strong or very strong, you may:

- feel overwhelmed when confronting complex situations, particularly when a quick response is required.
- believe that the quality of your work suffers when you cannot focus on one task exclusively.
- like to compartmentalize your work.
- organize tasks in discrete pieces to such a degree that you lose sense of the overall goals.
- rely on agendas, clear objectives and guidelines to run effective meetings.

Identifiers
People with this orientation may:

- become irritated when they are required to focus on multiple things and interactions at the same time.
- make an effort to sequence and structure tasks and work flow.
- compartmentalize and organize their work and personal space.
- display frustration when plans and projects have to be disrupted at the last minute.

Learning Objectives
Your learning challenges may be to:

- feel comfortable when you must engage in many tasks at once.
- develop a tolerance for frustration when communicating with individuals of a multi-focus orientation.
- learn to reorganize and restructure on short notice with ease.
- remind yourself often of the long-term goals of a given project.

Reflection

1. How do you experience this orientation?
2. In which situations do you tend to act on this orientation?
3. Which influences and experiences have shaped your preference?
4. How are the learning objectives relevant to you?

Dimension: Time

Orientation: Multi-Focus
Social environments that tend to expect, reward and reinforce a **multi-focus** orientation to time and its use emphasize the importance of paying attention to multiple tasks and relationships simultaneously.

Description
You prefer to work on a variety of tasks and/or relationships at the same time. You are not likely to be disturbed by unpredictable and unscheduled events. You seek dynamism in your environment and welcome change. You tend to be easily bored when you are asked to concentrate on one issue exclusively.

When this orientation is strong or very strong, you may:

- be perceived as scattered by those who do not share your orientation.
- appear disrespectful to those who expect you to extend your full attention to them.
- be bored and/or frustrated with people who focus exclusively on one issue at a time.

Identifiers
People with this orientation may:

- frequently engage in multiple activities at the same time, e.g., write letters while conducting a telephone conversation.
- bring up issues that are not related to the main topic.
- become visibly irritated when forced to pay exclusive attention to one person, issue or question for an extended period of time.
- express feelings of boredom when having to devote themselves to one thing for an extended period of time.

Learning Objectives
You may find it challenging to:

- develop a tolerance for frustration when dealing with individuals of a single-focus orientation.
- address discrete issues sequentially.
- see projects through to completion.
- respect the work processes of single-focused people whom you manage or to whom you report.
- limit the number of changes you introduce into your work environment.

Reflection

1. How do you experience this orientation?
2. In which situations do you tend to act on this orientation?
3. Which influences and experiences have shaped your preference?
4. How are the learning objectives relevant to you?

Dimension: Time

Orientation: Fixed

Social environments that tend to expect, reward and reinforce a **fixed** orientation to time and its use emphasize the importance of defining and managing time precisely.

Description

For you, events are critically determined and affected by time. Time is highly valued and needs to be controlled and managed. You think of time in precisely defined and discrete chunks. Punctuality is important to you. Good time management defines much of your behavior. You tend to view this as a critical professional attribute. To your way of thinking, planning and preparation are intricately connected to time. You take schedules, deadlines and commitments very seriously.

When this orientation is strong or very strong, you may:

- be perceived as rigid and inflexible by those who do not share your orientation.
- be perceived as lacking commitment to the overall goals due to your rejection of responsibilities and tasks that would change your plans and prior commitments.
- spend time trying to plan and structure events that do not lend themselves to such precision.
- easily get (visibly) frustrated and irritated with people who value time differently.
- often seem rushed to others.
- focus on the strict adherence to prearranged schedules but not give due consideration to overall purpose and context.

Identifiers

People with this orientation may be identified by:

- their frequent mention of and reference to time and time constraints.
- a propensity for planning and scheduling.
- the need to structure events precisely.

- their irritability when plans and priorities take longer than expected.

Learning Objectives
You may find it challenging to:

- see time as relative rather than as absolute.
- develop patience for business situations that are determined by a fluid-time orientation.
- build in flexibility when scheduling and establishing timelines.

Reflection

1. How do you experience this orientation?
2. In which situations do you tend to act on this orientation?
3. Which influences and experiences have shaped your preference?
4. How are the learning objectives relevant to you?

Dimension: Time

Orientation: Fluid
Social environments that expect, reward and reinforce a **fluid** orientation to time and its use emphasize time as a loosely defined and relatively abundant resource.

Description
You recognize time as an important framework for life's events, but do not feel the need to control and manage it precisely. You do not believe that time can or should be tightly defined and tracked. You tend to see timelines and deadlines as expressions of intent but do not feel bound by them during work processes and events.

You focus on what happens within time, and you let situations and events rather than schedules determine your course of action. You focus on the people with whom you are interacting and/or the tasks with which you are involved and feel that it is imperative to meet their needs before being able to focus on other issues. You have an open-ended approach to planning.

When this orientation is strong or very strong, you may:

- lose sight of time as a key requirement for organizational effectiveness and profitability.
- often be asked to justify your focus on relationships by those who do not share your orientation.
- be seen as unprofessional by those who consider punctuality critical to professionalism.
- frustrate those who rely on you to get work accomplished according to tight schedules and timelines.

Identifiers
People with this orientation frequently:

- emphasize the requirements of situations and relationships in determining business processes.
- treat schedules and timelines as approximate.
- show up late to meetings and turn in work later than expected.

- lack understanding for the frustration experienced by more fixed-time-oriented individuals.
- express a preference for spontaneity and a resistance to long-term planning.

Learning Objectives
You may need to:

- turn in work on time or establish new schedules when necessary.
- respect fixed-time-oriented organizational processes.
- identify the operative sense of time in a given environment or situation and adjust accordingly.
- develop behavioral routines that enable meeting precise deadlines and timelines.

Reflection

1. How do you experience this orientation?
2. In which situations do you tend to act on this orientation?
3. Which influences and experiences have shaped your preference?
4. How are the learning objectives relevant to you?

Dimension: Time

Orientation: Past

Social environments that tend to expect, reward and reinforce a **past** orientation to time and its use emphasize the importance of stability and continuity with traditions.

Description

You look to the past as a guide and model for your present and future behavior. You tend to judge plans and changes accordingly to whether or not they adhere to tradition. Continuity with the past is of great concern to you, and your behavior is guided by the need to preserve consistency. You have an intuitive sense of the importance of history and value the achievements of previous generations. You may experience change as threatening. You aren't easily intrigued by novelties and require a relatively long period of time to assess and evaluate situations and opportunities. Precedents and past successes are important in solving problems and making decisions.

When this orientation is strong or very strong, you may:

- be perceived as blocking or resisting initiatives to improve work processes.
- feel irritated and threatened by rapid and frequent change.
- overlook and disregard potential for critical innovation.
- be perceived as not taking action quickly enough.
- resist change although it is not in your control to do so.

Identifiers

People with this orientation frequently:

- exude a sense of stability.
- allude to past models and traditions.
- voice concern over a lack of stability and continuity with the past.
- display skepticism in the face of novel ideas, concepts and proposed changes.

Learning Objectives
You may need to:

- practice visioning, long-term planning and projecting that diverge from the past.
- focus on present requirements and strategies to optimize the outcome over the short-term.
- listen more carefully to potential advantages of something new before discounting it.
- resist blocking initiatives that require a change in proven processes.

Reflection

1. How do you experience this orientation?
2. In which situation do you tend to act on this orientation?
3. Which influences and experiences have shaped your preferences?
4. How are the learning objectives relevant to you?

Dimension: Time

Orientation: Present
Social environments that tend to expect, reward and reinforce a **present** orientation to time and its use emphasize the importance of quick, short-term results.

Description
You are guided by concerns over the present and short-term future. You are motivated by promises of quick results and returns. You prefer handling immediate day-to-day problems or crises. Your planning is based on the demands of the moment, and you tend to have a keen sense of requirements as they affect your business today. You are a skilled crisis manager and good tactician.

When this orientation is strong or very strong, you may:

- neglect the broad developmental view needed for essential strategic thinking.
- overemphasize the needs of the moment and neglect the long-range perspective.
- not fully appreciate the importance of history in business relationships and processes.
- be highly skeptical of long-range plans.

Identifiers
People with this orientation may frequently:

- emphasize present opportunities.
- seem rushed.
- emphasize immediate results, short- term profits and pay-offs to the exclusion of long-term benefits.
- seem irritated with or critical of requests for long-term plans and projections.

Learning Objectives

Some of your challenges will be to:

- recognize the significance and importance of history, tradition and consistency for past-oriented individuals.
- understand how the past has shaped the present and how it may be valuable for planning the future.
- practice long-term organizational planning with an eye to the past and future.

Reflection

1. How do you experience this orientation?
2. In which situations do you tend to act on this orientation?
3. Which influences and experiences have shaped your preference?
4. How are the learning objectives relevant to you?

Dimension: Time

Orientation: Future
Social environments that tend to expect, reward and reinforce a **future** orientation to time and its use emphasize the importance of trading short-term gains for long-term results and benefits.

Description
You are guided by concerns over the long-term future. You tend to base planning and problem solving on long-term projections. You evaluate the present by its potential for the future and judge ideas based on their benefits for the long-term.

You have little problem envisioning a future that is radically different from both the past and the present. Indeed, your actions in the present are often motivated by the desire to attain this different future. You welcome and frequently champion change, but only if you are confident that it will be profitable and beneficial in the long run.

When this orientation is strong or very strong, you may:

- be so visionary that you neglect the requirements of the moment.
- underestimate problems, crises and opportunities in the present.
- lock yourself and perhaps your organization into long-term commitments that may significantly reduce flexibility.

Identifiers
People with this orientation frequently:

- voice concerns about the long-term impact of decisions.
- are preoccupied with the future and articulate a long-range vision.
- exhibit high tolerance for frustration and are not taken off course by setbacks.

Learning Objectives
You may find it challenging to:

- focus on present requirements and strategies to optimize the outcome over the short-term.
- recognize the significance and importance of history, tradition and consistency for past-oriented individuals.
- take into account immediate concerns when you are considering a plan of action.

Reflection

1. How do you experience this orientation?
2. In which situations do you tend to act on this orientation?
3. Which influences and experiences have shaped your preference?
4. How are the learning objectives relevant to you?

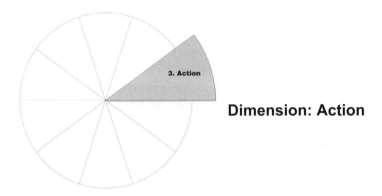

Dimension: Action

How individuals conceptualize actions and interactions with people and objects in their environment.

Orientation: Being

Social environments that tend to expect, reward and reinforce a **being** orientation to actions and interactions stress the importance of relationships, contemplation, reflection and analysis.

Description

In interactions, you are guided by a concern for building and maintaining good relationships with those around you. You are motivated by good, trusting interpersonal relations and expect that building such relationships is a function of time, experience with each other and incremental self-disclosure. For you, relationship building often takes precedence over accomplishing tasks quickly.

You may have a need to surround yourself with a permanent group of trusted individuals. When meeting new people in business, you require a relatively long "warm-up" period. You are careful not to extend trust too quickly. It is important for you that individuals establish their credibility and reliability. Before taking action, you need time to contemplate and reflect. You tend to scrutinize issues carefully. You do not jump to conclusions or take action quickly or lightly and you feel it is important that decisions are well-founded and well-grounded.

When this orientation is strong or very strong, you may:

- need a very long time before being able to extend trust.
- hamper your effectiveness on short-term team projects through the long warm-up period you require in social situations.
- be rather inaccessible due to a permanent group of trusted individuals that surrounds you.
- be susceptible to "groupthink."
- suffer from "analysis-paralysis."
- impede flexibility and responsiveness due to your relatively slow decision-making processes.

Identifiers
People with this orientation frequently:

- invest considerable time and effort in building relationships.
- are skeptical of unfamiliar people.
- approach new social and/or business situations cautiously.
- prepare their activities well and do not jump into action.
- require a lot of information and consultation before making a decision.

Learning Objectives
Your challenges may be to:

- develop a comfort level with making decisions and determining actions based on limited and/or incomplete information.
- focus on tasks and de-emphasize relationship building.
- engage in business relationships with people whom you do not know well when it is advantageous for your organization.
- be accessible to people outside of your circle of trusted confidantes and business associates.

Reflection

1. How do you experience this orientation?
2. In which situations do you tend to act on this orientation?
3. Which influences and experiences have shaped your preference?
4. How are the learning objectives relevant to you?

Dimension: Action

Orientation: Doing

Social environments that tend to expect, reward and reinforce a **doing** orientation to actions and interactions stress the importance of task- and achievement-oriented behaviors.

Description

In interactions, you focus on accomplishing tasks quickly and tend to emphasize measurable achievements. You are pragmatic in your approach to completing tasks, making decisions and building relationships. You view business relationships as functional; they exist to get a task done. Once your counterparts have signaled their interest in doing business with you, you extend trust readily in order to focus on the speedy accomplishment of tasks. You may not expect relationships to last beyond the particular task to be accomplished.

When contemplating actions and activities, you are guided by considerations of the quickest and shortest path to accomplishing particular tasks and achieving preconceived goals. You often feel that any action is better than inaction. You are generally comfortable with making a decision or mapping a course of action even when detailed information is not available. You locate required resources easily and tend to be a pragmatic, quick and effective problem-solver.

When this orientation is strong or very strong, you may:

- emphasize quantity of output over quality.
- approach relationships too pragmatically and be perceived as abrupt, cold, uncaring, or lacking in sensitivity and tact.
- overlook the importance and intricacies of building and maintaining relationships.
- easily dismiss the necessity of acknowledging and rewarding loyalty.
- neglect important details that may prove critical to accomplishing a task.

Identifiers

People with this orientation frequently:

- focus exclusively on "getting the job done" rather than on furthering a relationship with the people who are accomplishing a given task.
- end relations with others once the task that led to the relationship is accomplished.
- make decisions swiftly and focus on the speedy implementation of a plan.
- get impatient when asked to contemplate and consider issues at length and in detail.

Learning Objectives

You may need to:

- spend more time gathering detailed and complete information before making a decision or setting direction.
- focus on interpersonal relationship building and maintenance when doing business with being-oriented people.
- concentrate less on output and pragmatism in order to meet the needs of others.
- try to understand the significance to your business counterparts of long-term relationship building.

Reflection

1. How do you experience this orientation?
2. In which situations do you tend to act on this orientation?
3. Which influences and experiences have shaped your preference?
4. How are the learning objectives relevant to you?

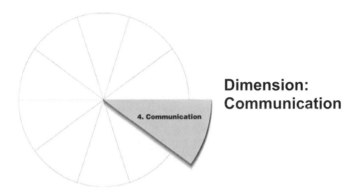

Dimension: Communication

How individuals express themselves.

Orientation: High-Context

Social environments that tend to expect, reward and reinforce a **high-context** orientation to communication emphasize the value of implicit communication.

Description

As a high-context communicator, you hold symbolism and propriety in high esteem and value behavior more than words. You are very sensitive to a wide array of situational components and tend to extract meaning from a wide variety of sources. You rely on nonverbal, symbolic and situational cues more than on verbal and written cues. You value the indirect and artful use of language and tend to imply rather than state what you mean. In order to get work done, you require a lot of contextual information about those with whom you are communicating and/or conducting business.

When this orientation is strong or very strong, you may:

- cause significant misunderstanding because of your heavy reliance on symbolic language and indirect methods of communicating.
- cause confusion among colleagues and counterparts who do not share your orientation and who find your intentions and expectations ambiguous.
- mistakenly assume that the individuals with whom you work share and understand your frame of reference,

which is particularly problematic in a multicultural workplace.

- create a high degree of frustration in lower-context individuals, who may see you as distrustful or lacking in confidence in them.

Identifiers

Individuals with this orientation frequently:

- distinguish themselves by excellent observational and listening skills.
- have well-developed interaction acuity and astuteness.
- are concerned with how others may interpret situations and often ask for others' interpretations of the same situation.
- communicate in a detail-oriented manner and attach great significance to nonverbal elements of communication.
- are conscientious and sensitive to the summary effect of all aspects of situations and interactions.

Learning Objectives

Your learning challenges may include:

- not interpreting low-context individuals as impolite or less savvy.
- identifying the ambiguous ways you communicate with others.
- ensuring comprehension and a shared frame of reference with your business associates.
- correcting miscommunication diligently.
- communicating expectations explicitly.
- focusing on explicit meaning.

Reflection

1. How do you experience this orientation?
2. In which situations do you tend to act on this orientation?
3. Which influences and experiences have shaped your preference?
4. How are the learning objectives relevant to you?

Dimension: Communication

Orientation: Low-Context

Social environments that tend to expect, reward and reinforce a **low-context** orientation to communication emphasize the value of explicit communication.

Description

As a low-context communicator, you value words and documentation. You explicitly state what you mean and tend to view and use language pragmatically and with precision. For you, successful communication is directly tied to the literal meaning of the words used. You tend to value the processes of choosing and interpreting words. Written messages and detailed documentation have more value and significance to you than information conveyed orally or personally. You need little contextual information about those with whom you communicate and/or conduct business. You place great value on good and precise oral and written communication skills and the maintenance of records.

When this orientation is strong or very strong, you may:

- find that your level of explicitness and reliance on written communication may alienate higher-context communicators with whom you interact.
- discover that higher-context counterparts may feel patronized or insulted by what may be perceived as "stating the obvious."
- be perceived as cold and indifferent.
- miss important information conveyed in a non- or extra-verbal manner.

Identifiers

Individuals with this orientation frequently:

- require that meaningful and significant information be recorded meticulously.
- are good record keepers.
- are prolific writers.
- ask for and provide explicit confirmation of their understanding of interactions and situations.

- show little appreciation for symbolism and metaphors.

Learning Objectives
Your challenges may be to:

- pay more attention to nonverbal, extra-verbal and overall contextual components of communication and assess them for unexpected meaning.
- acquire an understanding of the symbolic meaning of contextual components that are operative in a given cultural environment.
- try to use more visual cues when communicating with people of a high-context orientation.

Reflection

1. How do you experience this orientation?
2. In which situations do you tend to act on this orientation?
3. Which influences and experiences have shaped your preference?
4. How are the learning objectives relevant to you?

Dimension: Communication

Orientation: Direct
Social environments that tend to expect, reward and reinforce a **direct** orientation to communication emphasize the value of direct and explicit conflict management.

Description
You tend to handle conflict in a direct and explicit manner. You generally see conflict situations as impersonal issues that need to be addressed openly and face-to-face to reach resolution. You believe that conflicts can be positive and constructive and that most can be resolved quickly. Generally, you are not deeply disturbed when tensions run high. You appreciate the benefits of bringing contentious issues into the open. For you, direct conflict management is intricately tied to the notion of honesty and trustworthiness.

When this orientation is strong or very strong, you may:

- not be sufficiently attuned to situations in which it is inappropriate to handle conflict and contentious issues directly.
- be perceived by indirect communicators as insulting, insensitive and lacking in tact.
- underestimate the deep sense of embarrassment and "loss of face" that direct confrontation of even presumed conflicts or contentious issues may arouse in indirect communicators.
- feel comfortable giving people feedback shortly after a given task or event.

Identifiers
Individuals with this orientation frequently:

- address problems and conflicts explicitly and immediately.
- use words to identify and address problems or contentious issues.
- evaluate indirect ways of conflict management negatively.

Learning Objectives

Challenges for you include:

- taking care to avoid directly confronting business associates who may be embarrassed by it.
- increasing your awareness of the situational appropriateness of direct conflict resolution.
- enhancing your comfort level with the indirect conflict resolution strategies used and preferred by indirect communicators.

Reflection

1. How do you experience this orientation?
2. In which situations do you tend to act on this orientation?
3. Which influences and experiences have shaped your preference?
4. How are the learning objectives relevant to you?

Dimension: Communication

Orientation: Indirect

Social environments that tend to expect, reward and reinforce an **indirect** orientation to communication emphasize the value of indirect and implicit conflict management.

Description

You tend to handle conflict in an implicit way by avoiding direct confrontations. It is important to you to minimize the surface appearance of conflict and criticism. Generally, you see conflict situations as threats to personal integrity, dignity and/or "face."

Preserving and saving "face," personal dignity and integrity are overriding concerns for you in interactions so as to prevent possible embarrassments. You may prefer passive resistance or the use of formal or informal mediators (lawyers, arbitrators, colleagues, friends, etc.) to address, manage and resolve contentious issues for you. You believe that open conflicts are not beneficial to the parties involved. Openly displayed tensions can disturb you deeply.

When this orientation is strong or very strong, you may:

- project the impression of not having an opinion or wanting to take a stand.
- be approached with suspicion by those who find your indirect style difficult to understand.
- be perceived as dishonest, evasive, weak and fearful by direct communicators.
- prolong existing tensions and negatively affect morale if you refuse to resolve conflict openly.
- reduce or hamper a group's creative and dynamic energy in situations where confronting conflict openly would be an efficient means of releasing it.
- feel feedback is best given via a third-party facilitator.

Identifiers
Individuals with this orientation frequently:

- avoid making and addressing critical comments and challenging remarks in public situations.
- express their true thoughts and feelings about issues and people only to trusted colleagues and friends.
- implicitly or explicitly expect others to facilitate conflict resolution on their behalf.
- use implicit, nonverbal and/or contextual ways to communicate disagreement, frustration and/or anger.

Learning Objectives
Your learning challenges include:

- expressing opinions and sentiments explicitly when appropriate.
- confronting the parties involved in a problem or conflict.
- seeing direct communication as beneficial and efficient in certain circumstances.

Reflection

1. How do you experience this orientation?
2. In which situations do <u>you</u> tend to act on this orientation?
3. Which influences and experiences have shaped your preference?
4. How are the learning objectives relevant to you?

Dimension: Communication

Orientation: Expressive

Social environments that tend to expect, reward and reinforce an **expressive** orientation to communication emphasize the value of emotions, eloquence and style in interactions.

Description

As an expressive communicator, you value demonstrative expression in the workplace. In fact, work is an emotional experience for you. Emotional expression and expressiveness play an integral role in convincing and persuading people with whom you work to adopt a particular point of view. It is important for you to see emotional responses to work issues by your counterparts, subordinates and superiors.

You expect both positive and negative emotions to run high in the work environment. You may even require a constant ebb and flow of emotions in order to remain motivated. You tend to be quite animated in your use of words and body language and may even seek and expect physical contact with others. You evaluate the credibility and trustworthiness of coworkers and business partners based on their display of human qualities, which you associate primarily with an open display and expression of emotions and passions.

Style and eloquence may also be critically important to you. You may feel that the display of your personal and professional competence significantly hinges on your ability to express ideas and opinions artfully through the use of similes, metaphors and allegories. Your favorable evaluation of others may be linked to your impression of their stylistic sophistication.

When this orientation is strong or very strong, you may:

- suffer loss of credibility in the eyes of those who evaluate it on the basis of a non-expressive, instrumental or "matter-of-fact" style.
- find that your need for expressiveness and open display of emotions in the workplace can deeply frustrate and demoralize co-workers who are less expressive in their style of communication.

- notice that coworkers with a different orientation may judge your expressiveness and emphasis on eloquence as unprofessional and unbusinesslike.

Identifiers
Individuals with this orientation frequently:

- display positive and negative emotions openly.
- distinguish themselves through a high degree of empathy.
- make emotional appeals in order to convince and persuade colleagues and clients that their point of view is correct.
- appear spontaneous when it is not warranted.
- use rather complex sentence structures.
- respond well to metaphors and similes and use them in presentations and/or speeches.

Learning Objectives
Some of your challenges will be to:

- accept emotional detachment in others.
- restrain your need for physical contact with people in your workplace.
- find needed outlets for the expression of your emotions outside the workplace if they are not well accepted in the workplace.
- adjust levels of eloquence and artfulness to an acceptable threshold for your counterparts.
- tone down the use of emotion in presentations, meetings or one-on-one discussions.

Reflection

1. How do you experience this orientation?
2. In which situations do you tend to act on this orientation?
3. Which influences and experiences have shaped your preference?
4. How are the learning objectives relevant to you?

Dimension: Communication

Orientation: Instrumental

Social environments that tend to expect, reward and reinforce an instrumental orientation to communication emphasize the value of accuracy, control and discipline in interactions.

Description

As an instrumental communicator, you value factual, objective and pragmatic exchanges of information. Communication is problem- or issue-centered, impersonal and goal oriented. You prefer an emotionally detached way of presenting information in order to convince and persuade your coworkers and clients of your perspective on a given matter. You tend to have limited tolerance for displays of emotion in the workplace. Emotional expressiveness in others may cause you to doubt their professionalism, credibility and trustworthiness in business. You often see work relationships as qualitatively different from social relationships, and you evaluate individuals at work on the basis of their direct and measurable contributions to business.

When this orientation is strong or very strong, you may:

- experience difficulties building rapport and satisfactory interpersonal relationships with those for whom emotional expressiveness is key to determining trustworthiness.
- be perceived as cold, rigid and disconnected or lacking compassion and empathy by those who strongly value emotional expressiveness.
- underestimate the importance of sharing and processing positive as well as negative emotions in the workplace.

Identifiers

Individuals with this orientation frequently:

- use a relatively pragmatic and "dry" vocabulary.
- limit body language in business interactions.
- get visibly irritated and/or impatient with emotional displays in the workplace.
- show little appreciation for eloquence of style.

Learning Objectives
It will be challenging for you to:

- develop an understanding for the emotional needs of coworkers.
- build rapport by emotionally connecting with coworkers and business associates.
- empathize with others when appropriate in a business environment.

Reflection

1. How do you experience this orientation?
2. In which situations do you tend to act on this orientation?
3. Which influences and experiences have shaped your preference?
4. How are the learning objectives relevant to you?

Dimension: Communication

Orientation: Formal

Social environments that tend to expect, reward and reinforce a **formal** orientation to communication emphasize the importance of following protocol and social customs.

Description

It is important to you to observe specific rules of etiquette and protocol in the workplace and business situations. This need is particularly strong in your interactions with superiors. Likewise, you expect subordinates to be mindful of etiquette when interacting with you. You feel that observing decorum establishes credibility, respect and sincerity.

Overall, you see formalities, social conventions and customs as conducive to communication as well as to the development of business and social relationships. You feel uncomfortable in informal business environments and may perceive informality as communicating a lack of respect for you, your position and your endeavors. You see a lack of formality in others as indicative of their lack of professionalism, education and social graces. You tend to be keenly aware of the social structures within which you operate. You value respectful interactions.

When this orientation is strong or very strong, you may:

- be perceived as rigid and distant by people who expect a more flexible and informal approach.
- prefer conservative business clothing.
- have difficulty overcoming your aversion to informal speech, clothing, manners and forms of address in order to conduct the business at hand.
- feel alienated when working in an informal social environment.

Identifiers

Individuals with this orientation frequently:

- carry an aura of seriousness into the workplace and business interactions.
- dress according to formal, conservative or traditional conventions of the social environment.
- refrain from using colloquial language and adhere to rules of grammar.
- are sensitive to proper forms of address.

Learning Objectives

Your learning challenges are to:

- increase your comfort level with informal interactions.
- understand the value of informality.
- learn to extend yourself on a personal level when warranted.

Reflection

1. How do you experience this orientation?
2. In which situations do you tend to act on this orientation?
3. Which influences and experiences have shaped your preference?
4. How are the learning objectives relevant to you?

Dimension: Communication

Orientation: Informal
Social environments that tend to expect, reward and reinforce an **informal** orientation to communication emphasize the importance of dispensing with ceremony and protocol.

Description
You value casual, relaxed and friendly conduct in the workplace and business situations. You find that observing etiquette, decorum and tradition establishes an undesirable distance between people. For you, credibility, sincerity and trustworthiness are intricately tied to a friendly, casual and jovial style.

You see formalities, social conventions and customs as unnecessary and as insurmountable barriers to good communication and solving problems. You are uncomfortable in formal situations and feel alienated and excluded by those who maintain social distance from you through the use of rules and decorum. You may feel uncomfortable when participating in traditional customs and rituals.

You tend to value a free, open and uncensored flow of opinions and thoughts. You emphasize flexibility and spontaneity and an appearance of basic equality between people in a business relationship.

When this orientation is strong or very strong, you may:

- be perceived as rude, unpolished and disrespectful by those who value formal communication.
- unknowingly take away a necessary foundation for maintaining satisfactory communication if you unwittingly engage in informal communication with people for whom protocol and social conventions are essential.
- inadvertently and inappropriately transgress relationship boundaries (e.g., speak to someone as if he/she were a very close friend rather than a business acquaintance).

Identifiers

Individuals with this orientation frequently:

- are clearly unconcerned with protocol and etiquette.
- appear uncomfortable in situations that require observing rules of decorum and protocol.
- exhibit a desire to feel comfortable and relaxed in business situations.

Learning Objectives

Your challenges will be to:

- increase your comfort level with formality and social distance.
- understand the usefulness, value and social significance of formal ways of behaving in a business situation.
- familiarize yourself with the rules of etiquette and protocol in particular social environments.

Reflection

1. How do you experience this orientation?
2. In which situations do you tend to act on this orientation?
3. Which influences and experiences have shaped your preference?
4. How are the learning objectives relevant to you?

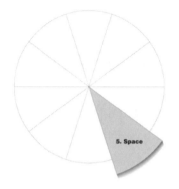

Dimension: Space

How individuals demarcate their physical and psychological space.

Orientation: Private

People with a **private** space orientation generally prefer to put a greater distance between themselves and others. Physical contact is limited, especially cross-gender touching.

Description

Private space cultures may place distance between people through separate offices, seating arrangements, or the size of the room. Private space cultures place an emphasis on closed-door meetings with minimal interruptions. People prefer to stand farther apart and tend not to touch during conversation. Private space-oriented people prefer a task-oriented approach to communicating with others and select locations that enhance their ability to problem solve and reach agreement. The use of technology for communications may be expected and emphasized for sharing information across long distances. Private space cultures may require more de-centralization and empowerment of individuals because managers cannot supervise the daily activities of subordinates who are separated by location, distance or geography.

Private and public orientations to space can also lead to a distinction between what information can be shared or not shared among members of a group. People with a private space orientation tend to share information on a "need to know" basis. Office spaces that separate people and job tasks may lead to less information sharing, even if everyone is connected through communications technology, i.e., e-mail, voicemail, etc.

When this orientation is strong or very strong, you may:

- appear shy, withdrawn, disengaged and/or disinterested.
- seem impersonal and lacking in energy.
- be seen as unduly secretive and therefore be distrusted.
- be perceived as inaccessible and unapproachable by coworkers and business associates.

Identifiers
Individuals with this orientation frequently:

- spend time by themselves and seek seclusion.
- avoid close proximity to and physical contact with others.
- clearly establish and define physical boundaries in the work environment.
- apologize when intruding on the space of another (e.g., "I am sorry to disturb you").
- feel a need to schedule appointments with people who work in their immediate vicinity in order to avoid disturbing them unexpectedly.
- refuse to attend or appear uncomfortable at public events.

Learning Objectives
Some of your challenges are to:

- stop yourself from expressing frustration and anger when coworkers enter your work area.
- feel more comfortable in social situations and public environments.
- be less concerned with the possible negative social consequences of your conduct.
- learn to disclose information more freely as appropriate.
- establish a greater comfort level with physical contact and proximity to others.

Reflection

1. How do you experience this orientation?
2. In which situations do you tend to act on this orientation?
3. Which influences and experiences have shaped your preference?
4. How are the learning objectives relevant to you?

Dimension: Space

Orientation: Public

People with a **public** orientation generally prefer to put less distance between themselves and others. Physical contact is common and expected, even between people of different genders.

Description

Office space in public space cultures may seem overly small, crowded and noisy. Public space cultures place an emphasis on open-door meetings with frequent interruptions. People prefer to stand closer together and tend to touch when communicating. Public space-oriented people prefer a relationship-oriented approach to communicating to others and select locations that enhance the development of trust and rapport. The use of technology, while utilized for communications, may not replace the need for face-to-face meetings or the informal exchange of information between people. Public space cultures may establish control over larger office spaces through the centralization of work activities and decision making, which ensures that performance and progress can be monitored.

Private and public orientations to space can also lead to a distinction between what information can be shared or not shared among members of a group. Public orientations tend to share information on a "nice to know" basis with those members who belong to their work or social group. Office spaces that group people together in one large room and require daily interaction and a sharing of resources can lead to more information being shared among others.

When this orientation is strong or very strong, you may:

- be perceived as intrusive by individuals with a private space orientation.
- find that others view your expectation of disclosure and information sharing as inappropriate.
- transgress important social boundaries and therefore be disrespected in the workplace.
- offend others when you had intended to express something positive.

- be seen as naïve by others who may take advantage of your openness in disclosing information.
- frequently seek association with business colleagues.

Identifiers
Individuals with this orientation frequently:

- engage in physical contact (touching, embracing, etc.).
- seek out public social environments.
- stand close to others when interacting with them.

Learning Objectives
Your learning challenges are to:

- develop the skill of revealing information gradually.
- understand the markers that distinguish public from private domains and behaviors.
- be comfortable with distance in an interaction.
- avoid physical contact, especially with subordinates who may not feel comfortable expressing discomfort with such contact.

Reflection

1. How do you experience this orientation?
2. In which situations do you tend to act on this orientation?
3. Which influences and experiences have shaped your preference?
4. How are the learning objectives relevant to you?

Dimension: Power

How individuals view differential power relationships.

Orientation: Hierarchy

Social environments that tend to expect, reward and reinforce a **hierarchy** orientation place a high premium on power structures and the recognition of power and status differentials among individuals.

Description

You assume that society and organizations must be socially stratified in order to function properly. As a result, you assume that everyone has a qualitatively different value, as well as different rights and responsibilities. Titles, ranks, position and/or age bestow authority and status on individuals who must be respected by people in lower ranks.

You may feel it is important to show respect and deference openly and acknowledge "power distance" by using appropriate forms of address that reinforce hierarchical structures and social status. For you, it is not acceptable to bypass formal lines of authority in order to complete a task.

You prefer to work in organizations that maintain demarcated lines of power and authority, and where work is performed according to the specifications of superiors. You require clear job descriptions that indicate detailed job expectations.

When this orientation is strong or very strong, you may:

- seem overly status conscious, pompous, or pretentious and alienate those who have an egalitarian view of social relations.
- feel alienated and have difficulties establishing rapport in an egalitarian environment.
- be disrespected by people who do not share your emphasis on hierarchy and status.
- ignore the fact that, for equality-oriented individuals, respect must be earned over time and is not inherent in a position, function or educational level.

Identifiers
Individuals with this orientation frequently:

- surround themselves with objects that connote status and power.
- tell a superior what he/she wants to hear; not what they really think.
- emphasize and display evidence of their educational achievements.
- use declarative or imperative expressions.
- do not contradict a superior publicly or privately.
- refrain from offering personal opinions about key decisions to a superior.
- express outrage when coworkers behave in ways that show disrespect for higher status or position.

Learning Objectives
You may find it a challenge to:

- understand the psychological role of an equality orientation in the workplace.
- develop coping mechanisms when you feel undervalued or disrespected by equality-orientated individuals.
- learn how respect is acquired and communicated in interactions in a given equality-orientated environment.
- share opinions freely/honestly with peers and superiors.
- de-emphasize the importance you place on status and/or educational achievements.

Reflection

1. How do you experience this orientation?
2. In which situations do you tend to act on this orientation?
3. Which influences and experiences have shaped your preference?
4. How are the learning objectives relevant to you?

Dimension: Power

Orientation: Equality
Social environments that tend to expect, reward and reinforce an **equality** orientation minimize power structures in an organization and emphasize the equality of status among individuals.

Description
You assume that everyone has the same essential value, rights, responsibilities and social status. You tend to downplay, minimize or even hide economic and social differences both at work and in your personal life. It is important to you that everyone is included and has the same opportunities. You tend to be sensitive to the needs of everyone in a situation.

It is acceptable for you to bypass formal lines of authority in order to get things done. You may also feel uneasy and irritated by official titles and forms of address that reinforce hierarchical structures. You generally prefer to work within a "flat" organizational structure.

When this orientation is strong or very strong, you may:

- not notice that others expect you to maintain an appropriate "power distance" due to their elevated status and position.
- cause confusion in hierarchy-orientated individuals who may interpret your behavior as unwanted "fraternization."
- be perceived as lacking a clear understanding of your status and role.
- be seen as rude and disrespectful or lacking in social graces.
- create great conflict and consternation in hierarchy-orientated individuals who report to you and may not understand your attempts to "empower" them.
- have difficulty assuming a position of status and authority even when it is expected of you.

Identifiers

Individuals with this orientation frequently:

- use open-ended questions when making requests of subordinates.
- downplay their own and ignore others' formal titles.
- start relationships informally.
- stress that everyone's opinion is valued.
- display irritation or even outrage when observing deferential or status-conscious behavior.
- feel comfortable contradicting superiors publicly and privately.
- offer personal opinions about key decisions to a superior.

Learning Objectives

Your challenges are to:

- consider the impact of your decisions and actions on others in the work environment.
- understand the needs of those who identify with and are motivated by collective undertakings.
- increase tolerance for situations in which individual choices are absent and matters are socially determined.
- de-emphasize self-interest and consider group or team interests more seriously.

Reflection

1. How do you experience this orientation?
2. In which situations do you tend to act on this orientation?
3. Which influences and experiences have shaped your preference?
4. How are the learning objectives relevant to you?

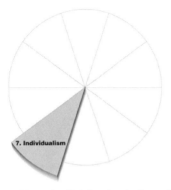

Dimension: Individualism

How individuals define their identity.

Orientation: Individualistic

Social environments that tend to expect, reward and reinforce an **individualistic** orientation emphasize individual motivation and personal independence and achievement as the cornerstones of identity.

Description

You are driven and motivated primarily by your own personal interests, accomplishments and potentials. You make decisions and take action according to what is best for you, based on your own wishes and judgment. You require and expect your environment to provide you with a great degree of personal choice.

You expect every individual to be primarily responsible for him- or herself. You see conflict between individuals' interests as the natural way in which they assert their personal interests, reach their goals and meet their needs.

You value personal independence, prize individual achievements and you expect to be recognized and rewarded for your own contributions and achievements. You value and admire self-driven, determined and self-motivated individuals.

When this orientation is strong or very strong, you may:

- seem selfish and inconsiderate to others,
- often underestimate the need for groups to process information.

- tend to ignore or overlook the productive potential of a cohesive group.
- experience difficulties working effectively in teams.
- alienate those who are primarily motivated by collaborative efforts.
- become frustrated and irritated with an absence of choices.

Identifiers
Individuals with this orientation frequently:

- discuss themselves and their motivation and interests.
- emphasize the first person singular when proposing ideas (e.g., "I think...").
- act and make decisions without informing or preparing others.
- decrease their interest in and contribution to activities when the personal benefits become less obvious to them.
- do not display consideration of the impact of their decisions and actions on others.
- view teams as a temporary collection of individuals.
- resist and object to predetermined structures and processes.
- maintain a loose relationship to others in their larger social environment.

Learning Objectives
Your challenges are to:

- consider the impact of your decisions and actions on others in the work environment.
- understand the needs of those who identify with and are motivated by collective undertakings.
- increase tolerances for situations in which individual's choices are absent and matters are socially determined.
- de-emphasize self-interest and consider group or team interests more seriously.

Reflection

1. How do you experience this orientation?
2. In which situations do you tend to act on this orientation?
3. Which influences and experiences have shaped your preference?
4. How are the learning objectives relevant to you?

Dimension: Individualism

Orientation: Collectivistic
Social environments that tend to expect, reward and reinforce a **collectivistic** orientation place a high value on the subordination of individual interests to those of a group and emphasize group membership as a defining characteristic of identity.

Description
You are driven and motivated primarily by your affiliation to groups and/or organizations. You make decisions according to what is best for your organization and determine actions based on their expectations of you. You prefer to make decisions by building group consensus, and you expect groups/organizations to take care of their constituents. You tend to experience open conflict within the group as negative and disruptive to group functioning and to avoid or minimize any potential for its occurrence. You value close interdependence and prize the accomplishment of groups. You are uncomfortable in situations in which you are isolated from the group, individually rewarded for your efforts or have to make decisions by yourself. You have a strong sense of loyalty to your chosen organizations. You assimilate corporate organizational goals and characteristics as your own, and you have a strong sense of social responsibility and obligation.

When this orientation is strong or very strong, you may:

- frustrate those who expect you to recognize their individual contributions and skills.
- seem overly dependent on others and lacking in individual assertiveness by those who expect you to take individual initiative.
- be easily frustrated and flustered by a superior or corporate environment that emphasizes individual accountability and decision making.
- dislike environments in which performance is measured on an individual basis.

Identifiers

Individuals with this orientation frequently:

- require meetings to process information and make decisions.
- do not determine an action quickly or by themselves.
- seek feedback from others.
- feel personally offended when the group or organization is criticized.
- show great concern for the impact of decisions and events on the group/organization.
- use the first person plural when referring to business processes, accomplishments and goals.
- defend decisions made by their group, even if they had no role in the decisions.
- view themselves as a permanent extension of a group/organization and expect security from the organization while offering loyalty in return.

Learning Objectives

You may find it a challenge to:

- feel comfortable doing something based on personal motives or in your own interest alone.
- make decisions by yourself.
- assert your own opinion.
- put your interests before those of the group.
- be held individually accountable for a given project.

Reflection

1. How do you experience this orientation?
2. In which situations do you tend to act on this orientation?
3. Which influences and experiences have shaped your preference?
4. How are the learning objectives relevant to you?

Dimension: Individualism

Orientation: Universalistic

Social environments that tend to expect, reward and reinforce a **universalistic** orientation place a high value on standards, procedures, rules and laws and emphasize the equal rights and responsibilities of individuals and/or groups.

Description

Your judgments and actions are guided by an abstract sense of fairness and right and wrong. You value the equal application of standard rules, principles and processes. You believe that everyone has essentially the same rights and responsibilities regardless of particular circumstances. Your sense of obligation is primarily tied to rules and not to individuals.

You dislike favoritism and value fairness as an essential component of integrity and professionalism. You expect people to submit to general guidelines.

When this orientation is strong or very strong, you may:

- be perceived as mechanistic, bureaucratic and rigid by those with a particularistic orientation.
- alienate people who expect special and individual consideration.

Identifiers

Individuals with this orientation frequently:

- refer to universally applicable rules, standards and principles when assessing situations.
- seek to establish rules and processes when solving problems.
- resort to formalized problem resolution (e.g., lawsuits).
- expect consistent behavior from others in a wide range of situations.
- strongly believe that there is one "truth" and/or one "right way."

Learning Objectives

Your challenges may be to:

- develop a greater sensitivity to the differential needs of various situations.
- meet the interactive needs of those who require affirmation of their uniqueness.
- understand the needs of business associates with a particularistic orientation.

Reflection

1. How do you experience this orientation?
2. In which situations do you tend to act on this orientation?
3. Which influences and experiences have shaped your preference?
4. How are the learning objectives relevant to you?

Dimension: Individualism

Orientation: Particularistic

Social environments that tend to expect, reward and reinforce a **particularistic** orientation value the difference and uniqueness of individuals and/or groups and emphasize the differential applicability of rules and procedures.

Description

Your sense of obligation centers primarily around your family and social network. You have a strong sense of your own uniqueness. Trust in and obligations to those in your network tend to determine your decisions. You are very loyal to the people in your network and expect loyalty from them in return.

You may respect formal rules and procedures for conduct but tend to think they do not apply to you. You value and encourage uniqueness and the careful consideration of particular circumstances. You tend to view norms, rules and procedures as expressions of intent and loose guidelines, but you may not feel bound by them. You value the ability to adapt your behavior and approach to the requirements of the situation.

When this orientation is strong or very strong, you may:

- be perceived as disrespectful and obstructionist because you refuse or seem to refuse to comply with norms and rules.
- be viewed as eccentric by people who are universalistic in orientation.
- be seen as showing favoritism if you change or bend the rules for particular individuals.
- be regarded as unfair by those who do not share your orientation.

Identifiers
Individuals with this orientation frequently:

- emphasize the unique and particular circumstances of a given situation.
- make exceptions to norms, rules or procedures.
- expect that rules and norms do not apply to them.
- accentuate their uniqueness through unconventional behaviors and/or accessories.
- visibly display their membership in a particular group.
- believe that there are multiple truths and a variety of acceptable ways of doing things.

Learning Objectives
Your learning challenges may be to:

- place trust in standards, procedures and rules.
- meet the interactive needs of those who require an affirmation of uniform standards and formalized problem resolution.
- operate according to rules in a universalistic business environment.

Reflection

1. How do you experience this orientation?
2. In which situations do you tend to act on this orientation?
3. Which influences and experiences have shaped your preference?
4. How are the learning objectives relevant to you?

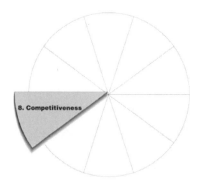

Dimension: Competitiveness

How individuals are motivated.

Orientation: Competitive

Social environments that tend to expect, reward and reinforce a **competitive** orientation value achievement, assertiveness and material success. The expected outcomes and projected results of interactions are primary motivators.

Description

You generally assume that employees compete with each other for recognition and rewards. You value achievement and results. Personal ambition and assertiveness are important to you. Harmonious teamwork, consensus building and the development of mutually beneficial interdependencies are not powerful motivators for your behavior and actions.

When this orientation is strong or very strong, you may:

- have a clearly defined sense of your personal strengths and contributions to the workplace.
- be very comfortable articulating and defending a personal opinion and expect others to do likewise.
- often take full responsibility for your performance.
- have difficulty extending trust to others.
- be perceived as too aggressive and confrontational by less competitive individuals.
- underestimate the need of those with a strong cooperative orientation for harmonious and trusting team and workplace relationships.

Identifiers
Individuals with this orientation frequently:

- assert their opinions and desires.
- emphasize achievement, results and goals.
- display and underscore achievement through material possessions and personal accessories.

Learning Objectives
Your learning challenges may be to:

- trust individuals, groups and team processes.
- take into account the impact of your goals and needs on others in the workplace.
- become less confrontational when appropriate.
- develop an appreciation for consensus building.

Reflection

1. How do you experience this orientation?
2. In which situations do you tend to act on this orientation?
3. Which influences and experiences have shaped your preference?
4. How are the learning objectives relevant to you?

Dimension: Competitiveness

Orientation: Cooperative

Social environments that tend to expect, reward and reinforce a **cooperative** orientation value interdependence. The quality of relationships and interactions is a primary motivator.

Description

You seek harmonious and mutually supportive, even familial, relationships with colleagues and coworkers. You expect to build strong and trusting relationships with work associates. It is important to you to maintain and nurture long-term relationships built on trust. You tend to be strongly team and group oriented and place great value on conforming to established norms, patterns and procedures.

When this orientation is strong or very strong, you may:

- avoid openly competitive and aggressive situations.
- be easily discouraged and frustrated by colleagues who see themselves in personal competition with you or other colleagues.
- be perceived as lacking self-confidence and conviction by individuals with a competitive orientation.

Identifiers

Individuals with this orientation frequently:

- emphasize the importance of process and balance.
- spend a lot of time building and maintaining relationships.
- avoid behaviors that make them conspicuous or that call attention to them in any way.
- seek consensus in decision making.

Learning Objectives

Your challenges may be to:

- make decisions without building a consensus first, when warranted.
- express yourself in ways that communicate self-confidence.
- enter into competitive situations more easily.

- define your personal needs, goals and ambitions before entering a competitive business environment.

Reflection

1. How do you experience this orientation?
2. In which situations do you tend to act on this orientation?
3. Which influences and experiences have shaped your preference?
4. How are the learning objectives relevant to you?

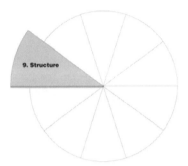

Dimension: Structure

How individuals approach change, risk, ambiguity and uncertainty.

Orientation: Order
Social environments that tend to expect, reward and reinforce **order** orientation value stability, predictability and the avoidance of risks.

Description
You tend to feel comfortable with clearly defined parameters and guidelines for actions and work activities. You prefer a precisely defined job description that explicitly states what is expected of you. You expect the work environment to be stable. You value rules, regulations and systematic procedures that are consistently applied. Predictability and security are appealing to you. You tend to feel threatened by irregularities, uncertainty and change. You need to avoid risk and seek predictability. Stability guides your decision making and problem solving.

When this orientation is strong or very strong, you may:

- be perceived as inflexible and obstructionist in situations in which others accept change and adaptability as the norm.
- be viewed as reactive and timid by those who value flexibility.
- seem overly concerned with internal matters – such as systematizing, organizing and structuring – to the exclusion of external business considerations.

Identifiers

Individuals with this orientation frequently:

- emphasize the need for stability, consistency, predictability and the containment of risk.
- require a lot of information, data and time for contemplation in order to make decisions.
- create elaborate contingency plans.
- create and look to rules, systems and structures as solutions to problems.
- are irritated, insecure and frustrated in situations that are unpredictable or ambiguous, or that require improvisation and spontaneity.
- resist and avoid change.

Learning Objectives

Your challenges may be to:

- increase comfort with change in environments that are very dynamic.
- feel more comfortable with unknown quantities and unpredictable events.
- improvise and take advantage of the creativity that spontaneity offers.

Reflection

1. How do you experience this orientation?
2. In which situations do you tend to act on this orientation?
3. Which influences and experiences have shaped your preference?
4. How are the learning objectives relevant to you?

Dimension: Structure

Orientation: Flexibility
Social environments that tend to expect, reward and reinforce a **flexibility** orientation value change, risk-taking and adaptability to unfamiliar circumstances.

Description
You expect the conditions of your work to change and are willing to adjust your behavior, activities and priorities accordingly. You value innovative and unconventional ways of doing things and are open to new behavior patterns. You tend to view change and risk as an opportunity for growth. You are not threatened by shifting parameters or unpredictable and ambiguous situations. You are comfortable in situations that require you to take risks, improvise or be spontaneous. You tend to value and strive for innovation and adaptability.

When this orientation is strong or very strong, you may:

- strongly resist settling into routines and structures, and underestimate their importance in team- and group-oriented work situations.
- be perceived as insensitive to the profound stress that change and risk can produce in order-oriented individuals.

Identifiers
Individuals with this orientation frequently:

- de-emphasize the need for detailed preparation before meetings, presentations and negotiations.
- trust their ability to "make things work" without preparation.
- emphasize the positive nature of risk and change.
- seek out innovation and new, unconventional ways of doing things.
- challenge the *status quo*.

Learning Objectives
Your challenges may be to:

- increase comfort with ordered and structured environments.
- understand the need for stability and predictability in order-oriented individuals.
- lower expectations for a quick pace and speedy changes when working with order-oriented individuals.
- accept that order-oriented individuals require more time and preparation in order to make change and innovation possible.
- understand the value to others of preparing for events.
- accept the *status quo* when it is advisable or beneficial to you.

Reflection

1. How do you experience this orientation?
2. In which situations do you tend to act on this orientation?
3. Which influences and experiences have shaped your preference?
4. How are the learning objectives relevant to you?

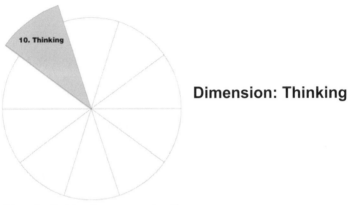

Dimension: Thinking

How individuals conceptualize.

Orientation: Deductive

Social environments that tend to expect, reward and reinforce a **deductive** orientation value reasoning based on principles, theories and abstract logic.

Description

You focus primarily on theories, abstract concepts and principles rather than on the details of a situation. In other words, your thinking moves from the general to the specific. You tend to evaluate the quality and soundness of a presentation and proposal based on the concepts upon which they rest. You get frustrated when the conceptual foundation is not readily apparent or sufficiently developed. You tend to scrutinize and debate conceptual frameworks and key principles before applying them to individual situations. In addition, you frequently introduce new ideas by outlining and discussing the underlying principles and theories rather than their application to particular scenarios.

When this orientation is strong or very strong, you may:

- be perceived as unrealistic or lost in conceptualization and abstraction by people who do not value this orientation.
- focus on scrutinizing theories, thereby neglecting the particular situation under consideration.
- ignore significant particulars in order to "fit" data to a theory.

- be perceived as dogmatic and inflexible by inductive thinkers.

Identifiers
Individuals with this orientation frequently:

- comment on, critique and question the soundness of theories on an abstract level.
- present theories, concepts and models before describing particular cases.
- de-emphasize application and implementation.
- get impatient and frustrated with case studies and anecdotes.

Learning Objectives
Your learning challenges may be to:

- resist "fitting" data to a theory.
- pay greater attention to detail.
- focus on the application and implementation of concepts and models.
- learn to value case studies and anecdotes in some contexts.

Reflection

1. How do you experience this orientation?
2. In which situations do you tend to act on this orientation?
3. Which influences and experiences have shaped your preference?
4. How are the learning objectives relevant to you?

Dimension: Thinking

Orientation: Inductive
Social environments that tend to expect, reward and reinforce an inductive orientation value reasoning based on experience, particular incidents and experimentation.

Description
You are interested in the details and particular components of situations and circumstances. In other words, you emphasize the specific over the general. You expect patterns and principles to emerge from situations and readily assume that they will serve as rough guidelines in planning actions and activities. You are generally detail-oriented and emphasize the careful analysis and interpretation of data. Abstract theories and principles mean relatively little to you if they do not emerge from individual circumstances and do not support a pragmatic approach to handling issues.

When this orientation is strong or very strong, you may:

- be perceived as lost in the details to the exclusion of sound principles and theories.
- underestimate the utility of theories, principles and processes.
- get impatient and frustrated by theories and deductive arguments or presentations.
- be viewed by deductive thinkers as lacking principles and convictions.

Identifiers
Individuals with this orientation frequently:

- focus and comment on the details of a situation.
- are interested in discussing case studies rather than theories.
- emphasize application.
- get impatient with discussions of abstract theories and principles.
- ask for examples to illustrate a given idea.

Learning Objectives

Your learning challenges may be to:

- appreciate the utility of theories and abstract concepts.
- develop patience with a deductive approach to planning, decision making and problem solving.

Reflection

1. How do you experience this orientation?
2. In which situations do <u>you</u> tend to act on this orientation?
3. Which influences and experiences have shaped your preference?
4. How are the learning objectives relevant to you?

Dimension: Thinking

Orientation: Linear

Social environments that tend to expect, reward and reinforce a linear orientation focus on the sequential and isolated consideration of issues and ideas.

Description

You prefer to approach issues and problems from an analytical perspective. A holistic, systemic presentation of problems and issues can be very frustrating for you. You tend to look for ways to identify discrete components and map primary cause-and-effect relationships. You prefer to convert issues into causal chains of events, each of which can be handled as an individual entity. You tend to articulate ideas, present proposals and convince others by presenting each variable individually and in a logically determined sequence. You assess the ideas of others based on analytical and logical soundness and get frustrated when these criteria are absent.

When this orientation is strong or very strong, you may:

- be quite pragmatic and concerned with analytic soundness.
- focus on actionable components.
- be able to concentrate on the details of individual variables.
- be frustrated and sometimes even "paralyzed" by complexity or systemic thinking.
- have a tendency to overemphasize the details of individual components to the exclusion of the goal of the entirety.
- feel frustrated by what appears to be an inability to conceptualize the relationships between components or issues.

Identifiers

Individuals with this orientation frequently:

- find the arguments of systemic thinkers lacking in focus and clarity.
- structure presentations by outlining discrete components and sequentially treating each one.

Learning Objectives

Your learning challenges may be to:

- focus on the "big picture" as well as the discrete components of a process.
- practice conceptualization based on synthesis.

Reflection

1. How do you experience this orientation?
2. In which situations do you tend to act on this orientation?
3. Which influences and experiences have shaped your preference?
4. How are the learning objectives relevant to you?

Dimension: Thinking

Orientation: Systemic

Social environments that tend to expect, reward and reinforce a **systemic** orientation focus on the holistic interrelatedness and integration of issues and ideas.

Description

You prefer to approach questions and problems from a broad, "big picture" perspective. You tend to focus on relationships between concepts or components of a situation. In order to persuade others to accept a proposition or argument, you point out the likely impact and effect on related variables. You prefer a synthetic pattern of thinking. Being mindful of the complexity and interrelatedness of issues is a hallmark of realism for you. You tend to find a linear orientation to thinking reductionism and naïve.

When this orientation is strong or very strong, you may:

- tend to present issues in a complex way that can seem clumsy and convoluted to individuals with a linear orientation.
- overemphasize the "big picture" and overlook important details.
- feel stifled or paralyzed by the complexity of issues before you.

Identifiers

Individuals with this orientation frequently:

- focus and comment on the interrelatedness of issues.
- emphasize the complexity of issues and their theoretical ramifications.
- find linear approaches overly simplistic.
- structure presentations in a holistic way by emphasizing complex interconnections between issues.

Learning Objectives

Your learning challenges may be to:

- develop greater appreciation for and patience with a linear approach.
- develop a more analytic approach to conceptualization.

Reflection

1. How do you experience this orientation?
2. In which situations do you tend to act on this orientation?
3. Which influences and experiences have shaped your preference?
4. How are the learning objectives relevant to you?

Armed with this understanding of cultural variability, a neutral and non-judgmental vocabulary, and a heightened self-awareness; the basic elements for conducting cultural due diligence are in place. Applying this understanding in our observations, conversations, and interviews allows you to identify the potential gaps and their consequences.

Appendix A provides a quick reference to the types of challenges most often associated with specific cultural dimensions (see page 165-168).

Practice Scenarios

The following scenarios depict specific experiences/observations about a different cultural group. Identify the underlying cultural orientations and the potential risks involved.

1. Joint Venture?

A major U.S. telecommunications company was working on a joint venture project with a Mexican communications company. On the first visit, Mr. Maddox, a senior engineer, headed the U.S. team. On the second visit, one of his subordinates led the team. Over the course of the next few scheduled visits, the composition of the U.S. team kept changing.

The Mexican team could not understand why different individuals would show up each time. The project was soon riddled with problems. The members of the Mexican team were reluctant to act on decisions and enact processes that had already been agreed upon because they did not feel they knew any of their U.S. counterparts well enough to trust them.

2. A Symbol of Success

At the conclusion of an intensive English-language training program for a small group of Argentine managers who were preparing for assignments in the U.K., a graduation party was scheduled. Senior U.K. and Argentine company managers, the trainees, their colleagues and families were invited. The trainees were asked to select a representative to give a speech in English at that event. Contrary to the U.K. trainers' expectations, the group chose the most senior trainee, even though his English was the worst in the group.

3. Erika's First Day

On the first day of her new job, Erika sat across from her new boss, Ms. Leticia Lau, and was somewhat perplexed at the issues her boss was emphasizing. Ms. Lau pulled out a complicated flowchart that outlined the responsibilities of everyone in the office and how each activity affected others. She asked that Erika study the chart and spend her first day talking to her new coworkers so that she would become familiar with their activities and how they would affect her work and vice versa. At the end of the first day, Erika was visibly overwhelmed, particularly since she had expected to receive very clear instructions on the particular details of her job, not those of others.

4. Outsourcing Relationship

As an employee of the Technology Organization, my colleagues and I are working with resources in India. We have been increasingly frustrated by significant obstacles in our working relationships. The differences between our Indian resources and our requirements as customers are putting quality, timeliness and cost efficiencies - and ultimately our reputation at risk. Below are examples of where we need help concerning our partners from India.

Our partners seem to fear or are reluctant to admit that they do not understand something. Some of my on-site Indian colleagues have informed me that this could be due to a fear on the part of offshore or newly-arrived-in-the-USA partners of losing their jobs if they voice uncertainty or lack of knowledge. The result for us is work done incorrectly and having to be redone. How do we ensure that our partners understand what they are to do?

They feel it is rude to challenge others and probe for information, especially with people of higher rank. The result is that they don't get the information that they and we need.

How do we make them feel comfortable in dealing with others and asking for more information? How do we challenge them and probe them for more information without offending them? Our partners spend too much time analyzing before deciding or acting. We are used to making a decision and immediately acting on it; they find this abrupt. The result is that we appear to be rushing into things while they appear to be making no progress. How do we ensure that they act on a timely basis?

Some of my on-site Indian colleagues have informed me that our partners may interpret words and situations differently than we do, resulting in misunderstandings. How do we ensure we and our partners are interpreting messages the same way?

Though intelligent and well-educated, our partners seem reluctant to speak up with their ideas. My Indian colleagues say that in general, Indians are introverted and shy. Also, they may feel it to be presumptuous to make recommendations to someone of higher rank. The result is that we miss out on potentially good ideas. How do we make our partners comfortable with volunteering suggestions and recommendations?

When issues arise they seem to prefer trying to resolve these issues themselves without informing us of the problem. We, on the other hand, believe in raising flags and doing so early. The result of their method is that issues may not become known at an appropriate time. In addition, when we learn of an issue and raise a flag, our partners interpret it as panic. How do we make our partners comfortable with openly discussing issues?

How do we deal with our partners' perception that men are superior to women? My Indian colleagues have informed me that this perception is changing in India and that increasing numbers of women are becoming educated and holding jobs. However, they say this perception of male superiority still lingers. The result is a subtle disparity in how our partners interact with men and women.

Our partners are deeply and personally embarrassed by errors. The result is that they become fearful of losing their jobs or being pulled out of projects. How do we help our partners save face?

To confirm the key cultural orientations and potential risks involved, open the link below and select the particular scenario: https://bookstore.culturalnavigator.com/cog

---

Key Learning Points: Cultural Due Diligence

o Cultural Due Diligence is *the practice to assess and prepare for the possible impact of culture.*

o It relies on a non-judgmental understanding of cultural differences and a well developed self-awareness.

o The Cultural Orientations Model™ summarizes the key aspects of cultural differences and provides a non-judgmental vocabulary.

o The Cultural Orientations Indicator® provides key insights into an individual's cultural preferences – a key component of cultural self-awareness.

Adapt or perish, now as ever, is
Nature's inexorable imperative.

<u>Mind at the End of Its Tether</u>
by H.G. Wells

PART 4

Style Switching

Style switching describes the skill of adapting to a different cultural context, situation or expectation through a behavioral approach, (i.e., style) that is different from one's customary approach. Mastery of this skill requires a clear sense of your own cultural identity, your general and specific flexibility along cultural continua, and a development plan for building a broad and flexible behavioral repertoire. This section guides you through activities and thoughts that enable you to style switch.

Ultimately, style switching is the ability to effectively employ a broad and flexible range of behaviors based on an understanding of the predominant cultural orientation in order to attain a desired outcome. Style switching should enhance your effectiveness in realizing your goals, communicating your ideas and successfully collaborating with others. It is very different from simply adopting or 'going along' with a different way of doing things, abandoning one's original intent or objectives in the process.

In a work and business context, the *Cultural Orientations Indicator* (COI®), is a key tool in this process. It provides insights that help develop:

- Cultural Self-Awareness – it identifies your personal pattern of cultural preferences.

- Cultural Affinities and Gaps – it indicates the general direction of your preferences.

- Flexibility and Adaptability – it indicates the strength of your preference (as mild, strong or very strong).

- Specific Action and Development Plans – it focuses your attention on those cultural gaps to which a different approach may best be applied.

Your COI® profile reflects the multitude of social influences and personal experiences that uniquely define you as an individual. In turn, you interact in a variety of social contexts on the basis of your culture-based expectations, assumptions and associated behavior.

This is illustrated in Figure 4. The inner circle in the figure below identifies some of the main social influences through which cultural preferences are formed. The outer circles signify the key cultural contexts/situations within which we interact and which have in turn exerted their influence on the formative experiences of our cultural profile.

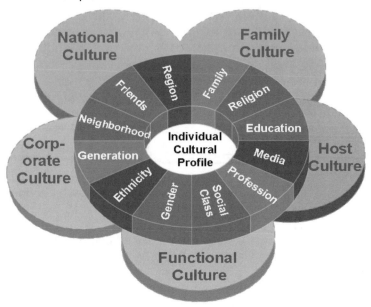

Figure 4 – Sources of Cultural Influence

The following activities will help you reflect on and engage with your COI® profile to realize these benefits.

Activity: Enhancing Cultural Self-Awareness

1. Select a strong or very strong preference as indicated by your COI® Profile and contemplate:

    a. Which influences in your life have shaped this preference?
    b. What has made it strong or very strong?

2. Select a mild preference as indicated by your COI® Profile and contemplate:

    a. Which influences in your life have shaped this preference?
    b. What has made it mild?

Activity: Identifying Style Switching Opportunities

To identify the potential value of style switching, analyze your own experiences and specific challenges associated with specific cultural preferences.

Complete the following COI® analysis for as many cultural orientations as you like. Two specific examples are provided as illustrations on how to use this process.

COI® Analysis

Step 1: Select one of your preferences (We recommend starting with a strong or very strong preference).

Example 1	Example 2
I am a Strong Particularist	Strong Preference for fluid-time

Step 2: Identify specific situations and circumstances in which you experience a gap (behaviorally, cognitively (belief), and/or emotionally). Situations may include: when leading a meeting, when doing a performance review, etc.).

Example 1	Example 2
Behavioral, cognitive <u>and</u> emotional experience: When I am confronted with a situation, either as employee or as supplier, where I am asked to comply with a standard rule, regulation or process, I get upset and reject compliance. Strongly relates to compliance with Six Sigma processes of clients, as well as using standard contact management systems internally.	Cognitive and emotional experience only; <u>NOT</u> behavioral: I am meticulously punctual at work, to internal and external meetings. I dial-in early to conference calls and am often the first in meetings because I know how much punctuality is valued in my organization. However, I am very stressed by this emphasis on timeliness; I do not consider it productive either. We stop a meeting when we should discuss more just because the agenda says we need to stop. Then we need to wait for another meeting to continue the discussion – it slows everything down – I get very frustrated by that.

Step 3: Identify the potential impact when you interact on the basis of this gap. Describe both the positive and the negative consequences associated with it.

Example 1	Example 2
<u>Internally</u>: My resistance leads to holes in the information concerning account and contacts.	My punctuality and timeliness has often been noted as a positive attribute. It helps me succeed within this corporate environment.
<u>Externally</u>: My resistance delays response time to clients; and may lead to missing details important to obtain project approval.	The frustration and aggravation I experience on a daily basis diminishes my motivation and causes me dissatisfaction with the way things get done.

Step 4: Explore how some of your specific performance challenges may be related to the dynamic you described in steps 2 and 3.

Example 1	Example 2
My manager frequently provides negative feedback on my negligence and disregard for common standards.	I get so anxious and stressed out when presenting to management. It absorbs all my energies.
David, my teammate, complains that he cannot get me to add information into the reporting template on time – slowing down the information flow and making resource allocation more difficult.	

Step 5: Identify how style switching (using a different approach) could assist you be more effective.

Example 1	Example 2
Reminding myself that standards help coordinate and expedite <u>all</u> our activities when I feel the resistance within me. Do these things <u>before</u> handling other tasks, not after!!	I think I am already successfully style-switching to accommodate the fixed-time orientation at work. Maybe I need to relax about it to not be totally demotivated???

Developing Flexibility and Adaptability

Individuals are capable of style switching along all the cultural continua and building a broad *behavioral* repertoire and associated skills. However, the energy associated with style switching based on certain preferences will vary. If the emotional attachment to a specific behavior or style is strong, the energy expenditure is greater than if the emotional attachment is weak.

This relation to energy is akin to a "personal energy bank." If style switching means the withdrawal of energy over time is greater than the deposit of energy, we may chose not to use style switching. Those cultural orientations that we chose not to style switch around tend to become "core" to our sense of cultural identity. Those that we chose to style switch around will become "negotiable" aspects of our identity.

The **core** orientations identify preferences and behaviors that are intricately tied to your sense of self. They are essentially non-negotiable. You can build an awareness of the potential negative and positive aspects of these preferences and behaviors, but you will not feel comfortable altering them significantly.

The **negotiable** orientations consist of those preferences and behaviors in which you allow a range of flexibility and situational variability. This range of flexibility does not threaten your sense of self. The greater the number of behaviors you ascribe to the negotiable realm, the greater your ability to engage in style switching will be.

It is important to recognize that the core and negotiable realms manifest themselves behaviorally and that they are therefore different from values. Because each cultural environment associates different behaviors with a similar value, building an extensive and flexible behavioral repertoire allows you to extend the very essence of your self. In fact, the negotiable realm is the buffer through which your intentions, needs, requests and decisions can be translated across cultures.

Following are two examples of people confronted with a situation in which either their core or negotiable cultural orientations were involved.

Martin Schutten in Venezuela

Martin Schutten, a native of Denmark, had worked at the local office for two years when he was promoted to product manager. With this promotion, he was expatriated to Venezuela to work at the Latin America branch. His role would be to oversee a team of engineers.

Unfamiliar with this plant and new to Venezuela, Martin had hoped that the team he was overseeing would provide him with a little guidance in regulations and procedures, etc. While he was very familiar with the product and expected that things would be carried out in a certain fashion, he also liked giving his employees the liberty to make certain decisions on their own, without always coming to him. This had worked quite nicely for him in his home office.

His new team of engineers, however, was not what he expected. They were always asking him questions that he felt could be answered without him. They made no decisions on their own. When Martin asked them about ways to change certain things, they did not provide suggestions. He was astounded that this team of educated workers could not give him any ideas or feedback.

His team members, on the other hand, were disconcerted by the lack of guidance from their new manager. They couldn't believe that their boss asked for their opinion or let them make certain decisions amongst themselves. They found that he was lacking in direction and confidence and they, in turn, felt that they could not function well without the guidance of a strong boss.

After a few weeks of ongoing confusion and frustration on both parts, Martin decided to seek the counsel of someone else. He contacted a colleague in Denmark who had lived and worked in Venezuela for six months, but was not affiliated with this present team of engineers. His colleague was eager to share information as he had also had great difficulty integrating into his Venezuelan team. He found that Venezuelans greatly valued a hierarchical orientation. They did what was asked of them without asking questions, never skipped hierarchical lines, did not enjoy and were uncomfortable with brainstorming and expected their team leader to have all of the answers. Martin's colleague also had a difficult time with these behaviors. But as time went by and he learned to style-switch, his rapport with his team was greatly improved and productivity increased.

Martin also enlisted the help of an informant within the organization who understood the organization and its culture. He asked his informer to provide tips and insights into directive behaviors that would make him more credible and successful with his team. In addition, Martin talked with other expats in the organization for any feedback and suggestions. After processing all of this information, Martin realized why his team didn't brainstorm or make their own decisions and why they looked to him for so much guidance. These behaviors were NOT what their culture expected, reinforced and valued. The engineers were used to being told what to do and were not used to contradicting or offering suggestions to a superior.

While he couldn't imagine having to give orders to his team and answer all questions without being questioned in return, he desperately wanted to find a solution. Every day, he observed his team, and slowly became a strong presence in their work area. He reinforced guidelines on a regular basis. He even practiced style-switching at home! He gave more direction to his cleaning people and asked his cooking staff to prepare something specific as opposed to letting them make their own cuisine decisions. In addition, through verbal and non-verbal communication, he let his domestic help know that he was the only one to make final decisions.

While Martin identified with the equality orientation and had grown up in a milieu where this was always emphasized and reinforced, he felt that his success as a team leader in Venezuela depended on his ability to style-switch. Although it was very difficult, he was committed to making this change. His will to learn about Venezuelan culture and to find ways to style-switch attributed to the success he had with his team. A short while after Martin started style-switching; he increased the trust of his team and was able to establish credibility and rapport with the team members.

Discussion Questions:

➢ What would be the risk if Martin did not style-switch?
➢ What enabled Martin to style-switch?
➢ How did he acquire this ability?

Diana Cruz: A Valued Employee

For six years, Diana Cruz worked for the same company. One of her main reasons for choosing this company was its particularistic orientation. She could determine her work schedule, set up meetings when she thought it necessary, wear casual clothing and decide, on an individual basis, the specific needs of her clients.

Shortly after she had received a promotion, her company was acquired by another. Her company was downsized and most of her colleagues were laid off. She, however, had been greatly valued within the original company and was not laid off.

Soon after the acquisition, she started having difficulties with the new management and company regulations. This company was very universalistic and had rigid policies and procedures. Diana had always valued a flexible work schedule to accommodate her busy personal life and odd working hours. With the new company, she had to comply with a set schedule. She felt that this was upsetting not only her outside needs, but also her creativity within the company.

In addition, when Diana wanted to schedule a meeting at her previous company, she would individually contact each person attending via an informal phone call, in-person or through e-mail. If she wanted to schedule a meeting at the new company, she needed to send a formal e-mail to all of the attendees at least one week prior and provide the meeting agenda.

While Diana enjoyed her work, she had also enjoyed the freedom, flexibility and consideration of her personal needs that her previous company had provided. She realized that in order to continue with this company, she would need to comply with a long list of rules, regulations and policies.

Shortly after the acquisition, she came to the decision that her particularistic orientation was a core orientation and she was thus not willing to style-switch. She felt that style-switching would compromise her identity. To the disappointment of her colleagues and superiors, Diana chose to take a new job that allowed her to maintain the integrity of her core values.

Discussion Questions:

➢ What was the risk if Diana had style-switched?

➢ What was the risk in Diana's not style-switching?

Planning to Style Switch

Style Switching is most required when we are emotionally least prepared for it.

You will find that style switching seems rather easy to do in the absence of specific pressures (time, deadlines, etc.) or when one is not vested in the outcome. However, it is precisely in moments when we are under pressure, feel stressed and are tempted to exercise our default behavior that style switching is needed most.

The following pointers will help you design your own style switching plan and explore some techniques for doing so.

1. **Notice when and how you experience cultural gaps:** The key to doing so is to track your emotional reactions to your experiences. Notice when you get angry, when you are frustrated, impatient, agitated, etc. These emotions are usually indicators of cultural gaps. When you experience these emotions, note the reactions and the specific experiences that "trigger" them. Be as descriptive and non-judgmental as possible.

   Please note that neutral emotions or feelings of happiness, contentment, satisfaction, etc., are NOT indicators of an absence of cultural gaps; as they do not take into consideration the reaction of your counterparts in the interaction.

2. **Identify the situations where you have most to gain from style switching:** Take inventory of the difficult situations you experience and identify what you can gain from style switching. You may want to refer to your previous analyses and reflections on your COI®; as well as feedback from others.

3. **Prioritize these situations and define your style switching goals**: If possible, do not make the most difficult your first goal. If you try to tackle a goal that is very difficult for you to attain, you will diminish your chances of success. Take a relatively easy or moderate goal as your first, build your

success and then tackle the next. Do not try to do too much. Remember that the most difficult aspect is often the ability to sustain a new behavior.

4. **Distinguish between behavioral and cognitive/emotional goals:** Remember that not all style switching is behavioral (i.e., external). Style switching may indeed most often originate on the inside, namely by employing techniques that help you manage your emotions or shift your understanding and belief concerning a given situation.

5. **Employ suitable techniques that can help you achieve your goals.** The following lists some techniques you may want to consider:

   Introspection/Reflection – This is useful to (a) identify situations where style switching may be beneficial and (b) uncovering the cognitive/emotional aspects to given situations.

   Meditation – This is a useful technique to shift your cognitive/emotional reactions and associations as well as to focus your mind on the situations that require more patience, resilience, or a different behavior.

   Modelling – This technique involves copying the behaviors of others involved in the situation regardless of your personal reactions or associations with the behavior. Simply "going along" with a given group can be a useful strategy to understand the specific cultural context and rationale. It also helps to identify the specific culture-based expectations and needs which are addressed by style-switching. Particularly in the initial phases of interacting within an unfamiliar culture, modeling can be a useful strategy to reduce cultural blunders.

   External Practice – This technique is very useful when the behavioral goal of style switching is difficult for an individual to attain and sustain. This technique involves identifying an analogous situation outside (external) of the situation requiring the "real" style switching. Because these situations are less invested with the "real" performance requirement, it may be easier to exhibit the desired behaviors; and mistakes will not have the feared consequences.

External practice allows you to become comfortable with a new behavioral pattern. Once comfortable, you can transfer the new behavior into the context where you will need it.

Peer-Coaching – When Style Switching is a clear performance objective; and a member of your work group, team or overall environment exhibits the behavior you seek to develop; ask this individual for help in coaching you in the development of the specific behaviors. Request feedback and practice from the individual and offer the same in other domains (if relevant).

The COI® is a useful tool to identify these opportunities. An indirect communicator, for example, may enlist the help of a direct-communicating teammate to develop a more direct style of conflict management. Coaching is usually restricted to bridging specific cultural gaps.

Coaching Program – This is a technique that involves enlisting the help of a professional coach to develop specific behavioral strategies. This is recommended for situations in which it is very difficult for the individual to style-switch, but where it is critical to the individual's success. Most often expatriates as well as executives transitioning into a different leadership role (different organization, team, functional unit, etc.) can significantly benefit from these formal coaching programs.

Cultural Mentoring – This is a more comprehensive technique than peer-coaching or even working with a professional coach as it involves assistance in bridging a number of cultural gaps and making a successful transition into an unfamiliar context. Cultural mentoring requires the individual to identify those that have a good implicit and explicit knowledge of the cultural environment and establishing a more formal mentor-mentee relationship. (See page 135 for additional information relevant to cultural mentors.)

Style Switching Practice Scenarios

In the following scenarios, style switching may be an appropriate skill to apply. For each, identify:

(a) How the individual would approach the situation based on his/her cultural preferences (What would be the likely risk?)

(b) How s/he could/should use style switching? (How would this strategy reduce risk and enhance success?)

Scenario 1: Providing Feedback
One of Frank Huber's employees does not approach her job duties with the thoroughness, attention to detail, self-motivated and responsive manner that is expected of her. Frank has to let her know that this is causing big problems for the entire department and that she needs to change her behavior to keep her job.

He is an indirect communicator who is equality and harmony oriented. His employee is a direct communicator who has a strong hierarchy and constraint orientation.

Scenario 2: Making the Sale
As a sales representative for AlphaCorp, Magda Bokovski is making a presentation to a group of potential clients. Her goal is to persuade them to purchase the new line of equipment the company released five weeks earlier.

The decision makers in the group are predominantly deductive thinkers and expressive communicators with a past orientation to time. Her personal preferences are inductive, instrumental and future-oriented.

Scenario 3: Improving Morale
The motivation and morale of Mr. Ahn's team is low and the team members need to be energized in order to meet objectives. The situation is serious. Mr. Ahn is preparing to address his team at a social event that he has organized.

Most of the team members are instrumental, informal communicators, future-oriented and linear thinkers. They value equality and are universalists. This pattern of cultural orientations clashes with that of Mr. Ahn. He is an expressive communicator, present-oriented, a systemic thinker and a particularist who values hierarchy and formality.

Scenario 4: Mediating Conflict
Two colleagues of yours seem to have a continuous conflict for several months now. Giovanni Montello is an expressive, direct, and informal communicator with a strong public and particularistic orientation. He vents his anger and frustration openly. Jacqueline Dubois is also an expressive, direct, yet formal communicator with a strongly universalistic orientation.

You are an instrumental, indirect, private-oriented communicator who has a strong universalistic orientation. You want to help both resolve this "never-ending" conflict.

To view suggested solutions to each scenario go to the following link and click on the appropriate scenario:
https://bookstore.culturalnavigator.com/cog

Key Learning Points: Style Switching

o   Style switching is the skill of adapting to a different cultural context, situation or expectation through a behavioral approach (i.e., style) that is different from one's customary one.

o   Style-switching requires mastery of one's personal cultural profile gained through reflection and introspection, as well as experimentation with one's comfort zone.

o   Building adaptive, flexible behaviors and skills along the cultural continua of the COM™ is not equally possible and obtainable; it helps to differentiate one's core and negotiable preferences.

o   Style switching can be difficult to develop and is most needed when one is emotionally least prepared for it.

"... to reach new understanding and, in doing so, to form a totally new basis from which to think and act. In dialogue, one not only solves problems, one dissolves them. ... We try to create a new context from which many agreements may come. And we seek to uncover a base of shared meaning that can greatly help coordinate and align our actions with value."

<u>*Dialogue and the Art of Thinking Together*</u>
by William Isaacs

PART 5

Cultural Dialogue and Cultural Mentoring

Cultural Dialogue is the ability to explore cultural differences and negotiate mutual adaptations through conversation. Cultural Mentoring is an extension of this ability for the benefit of another individual or group. It is the ability to help others with cultural adaptation and integration. This section introduces a recommended process for applying both these skills.

Cultural Dialogue

Cultural dialogue is the ability to elicit cultural insight through conversation, and thereby illuminate cultural underpinnings of behavior and performance, close cultural gaps and create cultural synergy[5]. This involves more than *observation* and *active listening* skills; it requires a better conversation along the principles outlined by William Isaacs in his important book *Dialogue and the Art of Thinking Together*.

He sees dialogue as a powerful means *"to create a new context from which many agreements may come. And we seek to uncover a base of shared meaning that can greatly help coordinate and align our actions with value."*

Cultural dialogue is a powerful tool to establish a new understanding and create a shared foundation for thinking and acting. It is a skill most effectively applied when style switching is unadvisable, unreasonable, unfeasible or ineffective. Particularly in merger/acquisition situations, joint ventures, and/or multicultural teams it is cultural dialogue that leads to common operating agreements.

We can distinguish two types of cultural dialogue:

1. **Proactive** - Conversations with the primary purpose of raising awareness and knowledge about cultural differences. This type of conversation is a proactive measure for creating an inclusive environment and understanding of differences.

2. **Reactive** - Conversations with the primary purpose to identify the cultural underpinnings of specific challenges that negatively affect collective performance. This type of conversation is a remedial measure for breaking dead-lock and addressing the tensions, problems and issues related to cultural gaps.

This ability to engage in both types of conversations is a critical leadership skill in multicultural situations. It consists of conducting a conversation in three distinct phases as depicted in Figure 5.

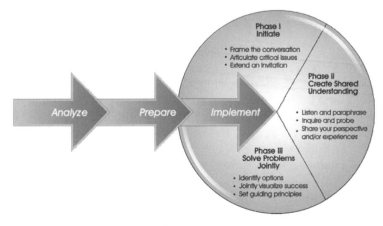

Figure 5 – Three Phases of Cultural Dialogue

The Phases of Cultural Dialogue

For cultural dialogue to be successful, the phases need to be pursued thoroughly and sequentially. Cultural dialogue critically depends on you pursuing the specific objectives of each phase and resisting the temptation to jump ahead. As a participant or facilitator, you need to keep the conversations in each phase narrowly focused on these objectives.

Phase	Central Objective
Phase I Initiate	Create willingness and openness of all parties involved to engage in mutual sharing, learning and problem solving
Phase II Creating Shared Understanding	To openly surface, share, probe and understand all positions, needs, perspectives, and expectations involved
Phase III Solve Problems Jointly	To *jointly* solve a given problem and establish operating agreements and principles

Laying the Foundation for Successful Cultural Dialogue

For cultural dialogue to be successful, particularly when it is reactive, we suggest to lay the foundation for its success carefully. This involves (a) careful preparation, and (b) creating an environment that is conducive for Phases II and III of the cultural dialogue process.

To be successful, establish:

➤ The rationale for using cultural dialogue,

➤ Clarity about the process and the objectives of each phase up front,

➤ The *categorical* distinction between phases II (understanding) and III (problem solving/decision making),

➤ The suspension of status hierarchies for the duration of the phases II and III dialogue,

➤ Ground rules, particularly for Phase II. We suggest minimally adopting the following:

- Assume positive intent by all,

- Listen non-judgmentally: be open and listen to others even when you disagree,

- Treat everyone in a dialogue as an equal: leave aside role, status and stereotypes,

- Search for hidden assumptions,

- Recognize commonalities.

Preparing for Cultural Dialogue

This worksheet below helps you prepare for a cultural dialogue and identify the success of your learning conversations in instances where cultural differences pose significant challenges. It will help you identify the statement of shared purpose, helping you initialize the conversation.

Guiding Questions	Notes
1. What do you observe? What are the behavioral patterns?	
2. What are your reactions and interpretations of this pattern?	
3. What are the underlying cultural gaps (use the COM™ vocabulary)? What is *expected, reinforced, and rewarded* in given situations or contexts?	
4. What are the *undesired consequences* for you and the parties involved?	
5. How is your interest different and/or compatible with the involved parties?	
6. How can you frame the purpose of the conversation by: (a) acknowledging the interests involved, and (b) expressing the desire to minimize *undesired consequences*	

Phase I: Initiate

Frame the conversation as a learning alliance of the parties involved – rally behind a statement of purpose that acknowledges and invites different perspectives

Articulate the critical issues – use the neutral, non-judgmental vocabulary of the Cultural Orientations Model™

Extend an invitation – use non-threatening, constructive language to "invite" the parties involved to a joint exploration and problem-solving meeting

---

Guiding Questions

1. What do you observe? What are the behavioral patterns?

2. What are your reactions to and interpretation of this pattern?

3. What are the underlying cultural gaps in the frame of reference?

4. What are the undesired consequences for you and the parties involved?

5. How is your interest different from and/or compatible with that of the other involved parties?

6. How can you frame the purpose of the conversation by:

   (a) acknowledging the interest involved?

   (b) expressing the desire to minimize undesired consequences?

Phase II: Create Shared Understanding

Listen and paraphrase - pay attention to the articulated and unarticulated messages. Verify and clarify by stating your interpretation and understanding

Inquire and probe - ask non-leading, open-ended questions and lead counterparts to make general statements concrete and specific

Share your perspective and/or experiences - differentiate between behavior, intent/cultural drivers and emotional impact. Acknowledge the perspectives involved - remember that acknowledgement does not mean agreement

Guiding Questions

1. What kind of questions could you ask?

2. How will you inquire and probe?

3. How would you share your perspective and experiences following the principles above?

Phase III: Solve Problems Jointly

Identify options - be creative in outlining possible solutions and approaches. Make sure that these options address the interests and needs of each party

Jointly visualize success - create and articulate both a general and a specific image of success

Set guiding principles – articulate principles that will guide actions and behaviors that all parties recognize as constructive

---

Guiding Questions:

1. What kinds of options could you envision as solutions and/or viable approaches? How would they address each party's interests and needs?

2. What is the specific image of success for one of the options you have identified?

3. Which guiding principle could you suggest?

Cultural Mentoring

While cultural dialogue is an important part of the cultural mentoring skill, it is a step beyond as it is a sustained focus on assisting an individual or group develop adaptive approaches in a new and different cultural environment.

Cultural mentoring is essentially the act of applying one's experiences and insights for the benefits of other parties. The cultural mentor is therefore in a role to facilitate cultural understanding and integration to a new and different cultural environment. Cultural mentoring can be applied to a variety of situations and circumstances, among them:

> ➢ assisting a new colleague in decoding the cultural norms of a new organization or team,

> ➢ helping two groups integrate practices, or

> ➢ coaching an international assignee in managing the difficulties of culture shock.

This skill amounts to utilizing one's own awareness and knowledge to bring about cultural integration and effectiveness within one's sphere of influence.

The steps identified in the *Cultural Mentoring Guide* will assist you in enhancing this skill and applying it to your sphere of influence.

Cultural Mentoring Guide

The following questions may guide in identifying how you could apply cultural mentoring in your sphere of influence.

1. Which behavior patterns have you observed? Be specific about the situations and circumstances.

2. What are the underlying cultural gaps?

3. What are the unintended consequences of this gap for the individual, group or organization involved?

4. What are the specific behaviors that could close these gaps?

5. What is the likely outcome from not closing these gaps? (i.e., not adapting the style or approach)

6. What can be gained from adapting style or approach?

7. How can you assist the individual or group involved in developing adaptive insights and behaviors? What is your mentoring strategy?

Practice Scenarios

The following scenarios describe situations that can benefit from cultural dialogue and/or cultural mentoring. Review these scenarios carefully and contemplate the discussion questions.

To validate your responses to the questions for each scenario, go to the following link and click on the appropriate scenario: https://bookstore.culturalnavigator.com/cog

1. **The Newcomer**

   Kohei Wada, a fifty-year-old sales manager, recently joined a foreign electronics company in Japan. Much sought after, Wada joined only after extensive negotiation and with a lucrative contract in hand. During his first month on the job, he diligently studied all of the documents related to his job, performed official introductions with existing and potential customers and distributors, and began extensive rounds of socializing with his colleagues and subordinates.

   Since Wada had come to the company highly recommended for his sales prowess, technical expertise and English-language ability; Jonathan Collins, the U.S. president of the Japanese subsidiary, was somewhat disappointed by what he perceived as Wada's lack of initiative. So far, Wada had not presented a sales plan or offered an opinion during any of Collins' team meetings. Collins was especially nervous about the upcoming annual corporate sales meeting at the home office that both he and Wada were to attend. Collins was counting on Wada to give the U.S. Americans insights into the nature of the Japanese customer and the intricacies of dealing effectively with the Japanese distributors scheduled to handle a portion of their product line. As the meeting time drew near, Collins' disappointment did not abate. Nor did an opportunity to discuss the upcoming meeting in the United States present itself.

Busy until just minutes before the meeting, Collins barely had a chance to ask Wada about his flight from Japan, let alone brief him on his participation in the sales conference. At the meeting, the discussion almost immediately turned to a serious problem the Japanese subsidiary was having with its main distributor. The international sales manager, Chet Harper, directed his inquiry toward Wada, "Well, Kohei, any suggestions? You know Japanese distributors better than any one in this room."

Wada looked at Collins and said, "I think Collins-san has much more important experience. He knows best. I am just a newcomer." Collins flinched and said, "Go ahead, Kohei, let everyone know what you think."

"Yes, Kohei," Harper said, "We'd really like to hear your opinion. It is crucial that we come up with a plan to solve this problem as soon as possible. We're counting on you to lead the way." Wada stared at his hands, refusing to meet the eyes of anyone in the room.

"I'm very sorry but I'm not prepared to give my recommendation. I am a newcomer and do not know enough to say anything." Annoyed and impatient, Harper focused on Collins, "Well, let's hear it, Jonathan. I don't have any more time to spend on this issue."

After presenting a possible solution to the problem, with no input from Wada, Collins was furious. When he caught up with Wada outside the conference room, he said, "Thanks a lot, Kohei. You'd better have a good explanation, because, right this minute, I'm not sure why the hell we hired you."

- What is going on in this situation? What may be some cultural gaps and issues affecting this situation?

2. The Metro Account

Metro has been a long standing and loyal client of NOVO, a recently acquired company by GloboCorp. The acquisition has Metro's Jacek Robinowski worried, despite reassurance by Marco Botarelli, NOVO's account executive. Marco insisted that for Metro hardly anything would change. However, others on the Metro account team did not share the account executive's optimism. They were clearly worried and anticipated the domination of the "evil empire," which had only recently announced that it is now a "truly global organization." There had clearly been a lack of motivation and energy on the NOVO team. This worried Jacek.

In a meeting with the NOVO account executive and a new GloboCorp representative from the United States, Jacek decided to put Marco's optimism to the test. He requested flexibility in timing of special promotions, as well as store displays due to an internal campaign and reorganization at Metro. In the past, these requests have always been handled with great understanding, cooperation and flexibility by the NOVO team; in fact, that made working with them so easy because they understood Metro and its needs so well.

After making his request and detailing the flexibility required, Jacek leaned back. Marco reacted as he always had. He tried to figure out a compromise and already proposed some changes and accommodations to meet Metro's request.

It was noticeable that Sandra Caspman, the GloboCorp representative, became visibly uncomfortable. She responded with the kind of Anglo-Saxon vagueness that disguised a greater level of discomfort and misalignment. She said "Well, before making any concrete changes, we need to investigate this further. Some of the guidelines and decision-making criteria for handling these issues may now have shifted." Marco looked at Jacek, then at Sandra. He said, "Well, I guess I will call you later after we check this out."

Jacek knew then that his concerns about the acquisition of his long-time supplier were well founded. Should he worry?

- What is going on in this situation? What may be some cultural gaps and issues affecting this situation?

3a. So Agreeable

You are talking to a colleague and she tells you about the following frustration:

I am so annoyed about them. I have little experience working with them, but everyone I talked to has a similar story. They are very agreeable, say 'yes' to everything and then nothing; no follow through, without even recognizing or acknowledging that something is wrong. For example, I called the person in charge of testing with an urgent request to compile the most recent results and analyses into a comprehensive report/presentation for my group's leadership team meeting. He has a dotted line into our group and agreed to the deadline I gave him. He was not too pleased about the short timeline, I could tell, but he agreed and promised to do his best with the report.

The deadline came and went and I received nothing. Because of the time difference that afternoon, he was already gone. I emailed him though. He didn't respond and I called him in the late morning the next day. At first, he didn't say a word about the report. I had to confront him with it. Even then, I only got an "I'm so sorry" and "there are a lot of projects and only few of us." Listen, we are all stretched for time and resources, but a promise is a promise. It's very unprofessional and he put me in a really bad position. I was furious. How can I rely and trust them?

- What is going on in this situation? What may be some cultural gaps and issues affecting this situation?

- How would you respond to your colleague?

- What should your colleague do about the situation?

3b. Professional Courtesy

You are talking to a colleague and he tells you about the following frustration:

I am so angry. These people are very rude and brash. I don't understand how they can operate that way and get anything done. Listen to this: A few weeks ago I receive this phone call from someone in the planning group. We don't really belong to this group and never get anything of value from them. She requests a report from me <u>urgently</u> and gives me a deadline. There is no concern about workload or feasibility or even contingency. The entire call was only about what s/he needed. I didn't know this person and I cannot simply change my entire work plan and rearrange my schedule for someone who I do not even report to. She did not even talk to my manager or coordinate through our department. This is a strange way of doing things.

Of course, I was courteous and polite and indicated that I understood her request and we will do our best and try without making a firm commitment. I thought s/he would get the message; but apparently not. She called me the day after her deadline just before our staff meeting all angry. She insulted me for not following up on my commitment! Can you believe this?

- What is going on in this situation? What may be some cultural gaps and issues affecting this situation?

- How would you respond to your colleague?

- What should your colleague do about the situation?

4a. Forecasting Dilemma

You are talking to a fellow colleague and he tells you about the following frustration:

It is absolutely predictable: I simply cannot get certain regions to comply with my reporting requirements. I get so frustrated when I find that they are not as responsive and committed as we here strive to be. I sent out the reporting requirements in advance a while ago. I followed up with an e-mail indicating the deadline and precise reporting format; and I get no reply or just resistance. I am so frustrated – some seem to not even understand why and how the forecasting process operates, - as if they would not benefit from it. In my headquarters' function I often wonder why the rest do not operate with the same kind of urgency and perspective that we have. It's so predictable. I never get the reports in on time, even when I try to provide a more aggressive due date and put more pressure.

- What is going on in this situation? What may be some cultural gaps and issues affecting this situation?

- How would you respond to your colleague?

- What should your colleague do about the situation?

4b. Urgent eMail

You are talking to a fellow colleague and she tells you about the following frustration:

I get so annoyed at these messages from headquarters marked as "urgent." Especially the most recent one concerning forecasting! –Forecasting? ... Under our conditions, with this persistent economic and political instability, how can I provide anything that can possibly be reasonable or realistic anyway?

And then, whatever I provide, I will be held responsible for in the end, making my group look bad in some regional meeting where nobody understands our business conditions here anyway. So what is the value?

In addition, most of the information they want they already have. I provided it to them before – of course, not in the format they want it in; but that is for their convenience only. Why do I have to put everything into their format if the information is not really useful for me anyway? And this is not even my job! I am in a customer facing role and in this already difficult economic climate, that's what I need to focus on – if I don't, there really will be nothing to forecast. I have stopped taking these "urgent emails" seriously and sometimes I respond only much later.

- What is going on in this situation? What may be some cultural gaps and issues affecting this situation?

- How would you respond to your colleague?

- What should your colleague do about the situation?

5a. The 80:20 Fool

You are talking to a fellow colleague and she tells you about the following frustration:

You know, my teammate is so typical! I cannot believe it. We have this aggressive release deadline and you know how nervous I have been getting because not all components are thoroughly tested and some features are not even developed. With only one more week to go, and so much to do, I am not sure how we will get things done. Even if all of us worked through the nights, it is simply impossible to get a high quality solution released.

We need both more resources and time to do this job right, but she is just not at all concerned and wants to release whatever we have. She says: "In the context of the on-demand strategy, the 80:20 rule is good enough. We need to get things out fast. When we are 80% there, it's good enough. We can always fix and upgrade later."

I simply do not understand this attitude. It seems foolish. Why should I compromise my professional standards and integrity and that of our company just to be quick!? And, doesn't on-demand mean that the solution is optimally adapted and responsive to the specific needs, requirements and situation of our client? I simply do not understand. What is so great about meeting an unrealistic deadline and creating an unsatisfied client? I tried to talk to her about this many times, but she just gets upset and repeats the 80:20 story.

- What is going on in this situation? What may be some cultural gaps and issues affecting this situation?

- How would you respond to your colleague?

- What should your colleague do about the situation?

5b. The Demands of On-Demand!

You are talking to a fellow colleague and she tells you about the following frustration:

You know, they just don't get it! I don't understand why it is so hard for them to understand. We are in the on-demand era and that just means change for all of us. But this teammate of mine is determined to resist change. She constantly points out that we should not release this product on time because not everything is in place and properly tested. You know, how can we compete in the on-demand world if we do not rigorously apply the 80:20 rule. We need to get things out fast. When we are 80% there, it's good enough. We can always fix and upgrade later. We are 80% there with this product, so we need to release it – that's quick and on-demand.

My teammate talks about professional standards and integrity, but it is really a matter of survival in a very competitive market. Speed and responsiveness are key. She doesn't get that.

This is why we need the right people to win; we cannot afford to hesitate or linger. We need to be aggressive and get things out if we want to dominate the on-demand era. Frankly, I think that my teammate refuses to understand this. We need to weed out this attitude because in the end it will undermine the company's strategy.

- What is going on in this situation? What may be some cultural gaps and issues affecting this situation?

- How would you respond to your colleague?

- What should your colleague do about the situation?

6. So Frustrating

Today you speak with your new colleague, Giorgio Monteverdi, to coordinate and synchronize details and activities for an upcoming negotiation. He is extraordinarily enthusiastic and, while he impresses you with his use of metaphors and his impassioned way of speaking, you are not entirely comfortable because you speak in a more moderated tone. In fact, as your conversation progresses, his excitement seems to increase steadily.

When prompted for suggestions and recommendations, he launches into a sweeping description of a grand vision he has for a comprehensive and highly innovative knowledge management solution. You feel yourself getting increasingly frustrated by the course of the discussion. You have hardly spent any time on the details and specific activities that need to be coordinated and you do not have much time. You know from experience that management will need to have everything "buttoned up," leaving nothing to chance. This is certainly not the time for new ideas.

Whenever you steer the conversation to the more important topics, it takes Giorgio only a few sentences to arrive back at his grand idea. You become increasingly impatient.

- What is going on in this situation? What may be some cultural gaps and issues affecting this situation?

- How would you respond to your colleague?

- What should your colleague do about the situation?

Key Learning Points:
Cultural Dialogue and Cultural Mentoring

o Cultural Dialogue is the ability to elicit cultural insight through conversation, and thereby illuminate cultural underpinnings of behavior and performance, close cultural gaps and create cultural synergy.

o Cultural Dialogue applies when style switching is unadvisable, unreasonable, unfeasible or ineffective.

o There are proactive and reactive forms of Cultural Dialogue, the latter being more difficult as specific cultural gaps need to be bridged.

o For Cultural Dialogue to be successful, a conducive environment needs to be created, particularly for Phases II and III, with specific ground rules.

o Cultural Mentoring is a step beyond Cultural Dialogue as it is a sustained focus on assisting an individual or group to develop adaptive approaches in a new and different cultural environment.

PART 6

Cultural Competence at Work

Cultural Competence is manifested through the four skills explored in the previous sections of this guide. This section summarizes the key skills and provides a variety of scenarios that allow you to apply the full range of awareness and skills, as well as the variety of tools introduced.

Figure 6 summarizes the key skills and their relationship.

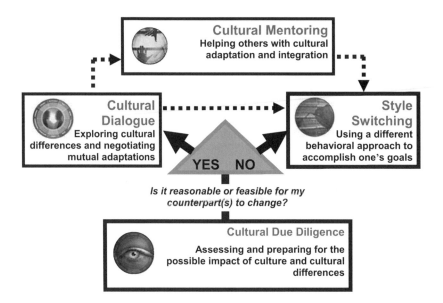

Figure 6 – Cultural Competence Skill Set

Index

Scenario	Issues Addressed	Page
A. Alejandro's Dilemma	Global Teamwork Use of Technology Forecasting	152
B. Relationship Management	Inter-organizational Production Outsourcing	154
C. Environmental Responsibility	Inter-organizational Client Relations	155
D. Delegation	Expatriate Effectiveness Gender Issues	156
E. Managing Upwards	Expatriate Effectiveness Gender Issues	157
F. Kula World Goes Global	Leading Global Teams Managing Global Accounts Expatriate Effectiveness	158
G. … But Everyone is "Committed!"	Global Team Relations	160
H. The Competitive Product Launch	Organizational Culture Mergers and Acquisitions	161

For each of the scenarios A-H, identify:

1. the cultural gaps that exist and may need to be bridged,

2. how each of the people involved may need to apply cultural skills, and

3. the likely benefits of applying the necessary cultural skills.

To check your analysis of these scenarios, open the following link and select the specific scenario:
https://bookstore.culturalnavigator.com/cog

A. Alejandro's Dilemma

Alejandro was an integral part of this geographically dispersed global team. As a field representative, he needs to coordinate his activities closely with the steering committee consisting of Suzanne, Jack, Philippe and Sean, the team leader. The entire steering committee is located at headquarters.

Every two weeks, Alejandro takes part in a team conference call. Since the steering committee members were located at the same site, they got together in a conference room with various field representatives calling in from their respective locations. They are all connected via the speaker phone in the middle of the conference table.

Alejandro does not look forward to these calls. He rarely gets to speak at the beginning of the calls. He spends most of the time listening to the four committee members' small talk conversations. It is not long before they monopolize the conversation, and their sporadic laughter and allusions alienate him from the conversations.

Not only can he not fully explain all his issues and concerns, he also feels separated from his team members. He attributes some of this to his accent and discomfort with colloquial use of the English language. Ever since the organization globalized, the ability to speak English well and know the many U.S. or British colloquialisms has become increasingly important. Although he manages to follow most of what is said in these conference calls, he has never been comfortable with English – foreign languages were just not his forte.

Over the past months, however, Alejandro's frustration has been growing. He feels increasingly disrespected and undervalued. Issues critical to him and his region have not been addressed fully and he feels left alone and unsupported while the demands and complaints are increasing.

Particularly Sean and Jack have been rather vocal about their frustration concerning his region's resistance to the new forecasting requirements and standards initiated from headquarters. They insist that these requirements are to "*create smarter, speedier and simpler processes."* However, they do not even try to understand that in Alejandro's region, forecasting was done very differently, if at all. People see the forecast as an unattainable goal that will never be accomplished.

His colleague in Argentina always says: "In Argentina anything can happen anytime. How can I forecast and be held accountable for it in some "global" meeting?"

When he tries to explain this in one of the global calls, he cannot even complete more than two sentences before some disparaging remarks are made. Alejandro always thought it ironic that a company could "globalize" and be so bluntly disinterested in neither what is important locally nor give him the opportunity to fully explain the local perspectives in a foreign language. Perhaps his friends are right: *Globalization is Americanization!*

To analyze this scenario and apply the cultural awareness and skills presented in this Guide, refer to the guidelines on page 151.

B. Relationship Management

Your company, in line with its strategic direction to concentrate on its core business, has outsourced manufacturing of the PowerPac component to the AREDON Corporation. This arrangement reduces production cost and increases speed as AREDON is specialized in the required manufacturing processes.

As profit margins for PowerPac have dropped significantly over the past two years due to fierce global competition, your company's competitive advantage is linked to both price and speed. AREDON's manufacturing capabilities in key low-cost international locations provide a good solution.

You are the AREDON manager and have become frustrated with the diminishing profit margins as your company has increased its demand for cost reduction. For AREDON, this large account is not a profitable undertaking and your boss has made it very clear that this trend cannot continue. You and your company, however, value the relationship with your company and have done everything in your power to adjust various processes, including waste management, to make up diminishing returns. The most recent request for cost reduction from your company, however, is impossible to accommodate.

The alliance manager from your company is a **doing** oriented, **direct** communicator with strong **universalist, cooperative**, and **deductive** orientations. The AREDON counterpart is **being** oriented, **indirect** communicator with strong **particularist, cooperative**, and **deductive** orientations.

To analyze this scenario and apply the cultural awareness and skills presented in this Guide, refer to the guidelines on page 151.

C. Environmental Responsibility

Your company in line with its strategic direction to concentrate on its core business has outsourced manufacturing of the PowerPac component to ARENDON Corporation. This arrangement reduces production cost and increases speed as AREDON is specialized in the manufacturing processes required.

As profit margins for PowerPac have dropped significantly over the past two years due to fierce global competition, your company's competitive advantage is linked to both price and speed. AREDON's manufacturing capabilities in key low-cost international locations provide a good solution.

The alliance manager from your company is a **doing**-oriented, **direct** communicator with strong **universalist, cooperative**, and **deductive** orientations. The ARENDON counterpart is a **being** oriented, **indirect** communicator, with strong **particularist, cooperative**, and **deductive** orientations.

Recently, ARENDON has received media attention for environmentally questionable waste management practices in two locations. Although local laws were not violated, the practices nevertheless are raising concerns among the environmentalist groups in North America and Europe. Because recent newspaper articles have implicated your company, there is great concern about possible damage to the global image of the company. AREDON, on the other hand, has been a loyal and accommodating supplier whose competence and expertise have helped your company maintain a global leadership position with PowerPac.

To analyze this scenario and apply the cultural awareness and skills presented in this Guide, refer to the guidelines on page 151.

D. Delegation

You are a recent expatriate responsible for managing customer support. After transferring in-country, you felt firsthand the reactions of some male managers to your role as a female manager. You want to change that, but also want to be sensitive to the local culture.

You have one female manager reporting to you. She is the least experienced manager you have. You want to make sure that she succeeds and have carefully selected assignments that offer her experience but little risk of failure. You're grooming her for a possible division assignment. You have talked to her formally and informally about her job and career. She's always positive and likes her work. However, you have a sense that she's not really happy. You think she might not be giving you direct feedback because she comes from a culture that emphasizes **Harmony, Constraint, Cooperation** and **Hierarchy.**

You've also picked up some signs that male colleagues think you're being too easy with your female manager. You want to give her tougher assignments but don't want to jeopardize her chance to succeed. If she were to fail in any way, it could hurt other women. What should you do?

To analyze this scenario and apply the cultural awareness and skills presented in this Guide, refer to the guidelines on page 151.

E. Managing Upwards

You are the only female customer support manager in your country. You report to a female manager who is an expatriate. You expected that, being a woman, she would be supportive of your career. However, she has tended to give key assignments to your male colleagues and relegated you to less important accounts. This is hurting your career and reinforces some people's views of the work women should do. You have indicated your dissatisfaction to your manager in many ways, but she doesn't seem to understand.

Your manager is from a different culture, and you think that might be part of the problem. You compared your cultures:

Your Cultural Orientations   **Her Cultural Orientations**

Harmony & Constraint   Control
Being   Doing
High Context & Indirect   Low Context & Direct
Deductive   Inductive

To analyze this scenario and apply the cultural awareness and skills presented in this Guide, refer to the guidelines on page 151.

F. Kula World Goes Global

Having operated as a typical multinational organization for the past 70 years, Kula World is now committed to building an increasingly global organization. The rapid growth of global accounts has prompted the company to restructure operations in order to service global clients better and more cost-effectively, as well as leverage the advantages of global sourcing and manufacturing opportunities. This means that Kula World has created global centers of excellence, operates as a matrix organization and relies significantly on global, cross-functional teams.

For Karen Gilberts, a long time employee from the U.K., all this translates into formidable challenges. She has been appointed leader of a core team of six. Their mission is to grow Kula Word's most important global account, Japan's Nagadoshi Industries.

1. **Jackie O'Dell** from U.S. headquarters who has been supporting the client in the Americas region.

2. **John Kazuho**, a Japanese-American from Oakland, California, who was recently promoted to Key Account Executive for the client and started his first expatriate assignment in Tokyo only three months ago.

3. **Suguna Kumar,** from Bangalore, India, heads a new team of software engineers in Bangalore who design applications for Kula World.

4. **Carlos Jimenez Castillo** from Juarez, Mexico, manages the production plant in Juarez.

5. **Heinrich Schwartzkopf**, from Germany, is the Director of Research and Development.

6. **Antonio Zanco**, Regional Marketing Director, originally from Italy, now in the midst of a two-year expatriate assignment and based in Singapore.

Karen is concerned about the cultural issues that could emerge between people from such diverse backgrounds. She has had experience with cross-cultural teams in Europe, which was quite a struggle, but a team this diverse is new to her. Although she is familiar with some team members, she has not met everyone yet. In fact, it isn't really even a team yet, rather a group of individuals with varying roles and responsibilities. Creating a team is up to her.

To analyze this scenario and apply the cultural awareness and skills presented in this Guide, refer to the guidelines on page 151.

G. ...But Everyone is "Committed!"

This is your first conversation with Gudrun Schönfeld in the German office. You are calling to obtain the perspective of the German team regarding the operation of the SYNTHOS team. You know things are not going well. The team performance is mediocre at best and a number of deadlines were missed. Key stakeholders have lost confidence and some are considering dissolving the team altogether. The team leader and the U.S. and U.K. teams are complaining about the German team being too rigid and inflexible, stifling the team overall with slow reaction times, insistence on established processes over responsive solutions and overt conflict behavior. Your job is to figure out whether, and how, this team can get back on track.

Gudrun complains about voice mail in the U.K. and the U.S. ambiguous e-mail messages. "It is very hard to speak to anyone," she says. "We receive messages that we don't quite understand, and no one gives us more background or specifications. We call and get an answering machine that tells us to contact someone else's answering machine. It is very frustrating!"

She continues, "Also, our Anglo-Saxon colleagues seem to assume that just because an e-mail moves a message quickly, providing the correct response and gathering the right information must take less time. I don't understand this. How can we work together like this?"

You decide just to listen. There is obviously a great deal of frustration underneath the surface of this 'iceberg.' "The worst," she explains, "is the double-talk and mixed messages. We have had two off-site meetings to work out our differences. Every time we develop great flip-charts and ideas, everyone professes their "commitment," and then we find out that the German team is the only team to act on our resolutions. Our Anglo-Saxon colleagues then tell us that some parameters have changed and that a commitment means that everyone will do their best. What kind of a commitment is this? To add insult to injury both complain, behind our backs, about the rigid 'German team.' How long will we have to pay for our history, I wonder?"

To analyze this scenario and apply the cultural awareness and skills presented in this Guide, refer to the guidelines on page 151.

H. The Competitive Product Launch

The launch of the Xetral Turbo upgrade is the biggest initiative of the year for the Grevier Business Unit (GBU), which was formed after the acquisition of Grevier by the Piergarten conglomerate.

Leadership has given the GBU clear direction that delivery of the upgrade success measures is critical to meet the business unit's overall growth and profit targets this year. The timelines have been very aggressive, but the organization has worked extremely hard to meet the 1st quarter launch goal.

All of Piergarten's Market Development Groups (PMDG) - which coordinate and execute all launches for the conglomerate by key markets - have agreed to the 1st quarter launch schedule, except for the two biggest; namely North America (NA) and Western Europe (WE). There are major launches by other business units scheduled in the 1st quarter; therefore there is not enough organizational capacity or market spending to support the Grevier initiative. Grevier's growth and profit targets will be in jeopardy if the large NA and WE MDGs do not launch early in the year.

The Perspective of Christina, Global MDG

"Five years ago, when Piergarten announced the 2005 restructuring, I was asked to lead Marketing for the Latin America MDG. It was a very difficult transition. Nobody knew how to make the business unit - MDG interface work. It took a couple of years, the right mix of disciplined planning and intense collaboration with the GBUs at the right interfaces in the system. At first they saw us as the enemy, but over time and with persistent communication and a lot of face time, we made it work.

I am proud of what I have accomplished. We literally brought order into sheer chaos. We had to learn how to deliver superior results and meet all the GBU needs, though not always their wants. It was extremely hard work because we were changing mindsets and behaviors one person at a time. It was the subtle work that stands behind the re-drawing of organization charts.

I guess we delivered and my efforts did not go unnoticed. They offered me an opportunity at the G.O. A year and a half ago, I moved to headquarters to work in the Global MDG. It was a difficult adjustment for me and my family, but we have come to like it. We are still getting used to living in the United States. Working here is also a little different from what I had expected. People are very polite and kind and my ability to quietly build consensus behind the scenes has headed off many potential conflicts. However, I seldom feel like I connect with my colleagues at a deeper level like I did at home.

They look at what we did in Latin America as a best practice. That makes me proud. In my current role, I am helping to transfer learning and Latin American practices to other MDGs. One advantage we have in the Latin American region is that it is such a tightly knit network of relationships. That makes coordinating and planning a breeze. Other regions are not so fortunate.

The integration of the Grevier GBU has been absorbing a lot of my time, more than I can reasonably spare. I have been trying to coach Benoit and his people on how to navigate the planning process but he is not at all responsive and this really frustrates me. My schedule is tight as it is and he keeps asking me to change the NA and WE 1st quarter initiative schedules without listening to my response.

I sent several e-mails with advice on whom to speak with and what data to present to work with the system, but he doesn't seem to be following any of it. I even sent templates and samples for him to review and complete. All he needs to do is read and follow the steps outlined. I wish we had all this so clearly defined and documented when we started the change in Latin America. Benoit is lucky! It could be a lot more chaotic. He just needs to follow the process. Perhaps he is just resisting the integration! He should get over it; now it's about delivering coordinated results, not his needs.

Benoit requested a meeting today. I really don't know what else I can tell him! It is not a good time for me right now as I am handling an enormous number of projects. I really don't want to waste my time hand-holding him through the process if all he needs to do is read and follow it. It is really frustrating...."

The Perspective of Benoit, Grevier Business Unit (GBU)

"My decision to join Grevier six years ago turned out to be a good move. I wasn't sure if consumer products was for me, but the Grevier recruiters convinced me that my marketing skills and past industrial experience would be a good fit. My wife and children were happy that we were able to stay close to our families.

Early on, my quick decision-making style and clear direction-setting helped me to stand out and succeed here. Grevier has good systems in place for managing the base business. I especially like the fact that when a big idea or opportunity comes up, I can bypass the system and make it happen. A couple of those big ideas have been the business-building highlights of my career. I have coached my top managers to do the same.

I had my doubts about the merger with Piergarten. I've heard about their way of doing things and I wasn't sure if my style would be appreciated. However, senior management from both Grevier and Piergarten convinced me that I would be valued and that if I continued to perform, there would be even better opportunities for advancement within the new organization. That sounded good so I stayed, even though some of my peers decided to leave.

The annual performance targets are challenging – that hasn't changed! We have great initiatives in place, but the execution is not going so smoothly. The MDGs in WE and NA will not budge on the 1st quarter schedule. I had my organization fill out the endless templates and planning documents and I have tried to appeal directly to Christina in the Global MDG but she never answers. She just keeps sending me e-mails with forms and referring me to different people in different functions.

Time is getting tight; I don't know how they expect me to run my business! At Grevier, we never missed a launch – that would have been sacrilegious. Why does Piergarten set these aggressive targets only to put obstacles in the way of achieving them? It doesn't make sense. If Christina would just call, we could get on with it. I am getting frustrated and tired of being brushed off. She has finally agreed to meet me in person. I'm going to headquarters to meet her and cut through all this bureaucracy..."

To analyze this scenario and apply the cultural awareness and skills presented in this Guide, refer to the guidelines on page 151.

Key Learning Points:
Cultural Competence at Work

o   Cultural Competence requires the ability to assess and prepare for the possible impact of culture and to judiciously identify how style switching, cultural dialogue and cultural mentoring need to be applied in order to achieve desired outcomes.

o   Lack of care in cultural due diligence can and often does lead to unwarranted assumptions about situations, motivations and counterparts that strain relationships and outcomes.

o   The ability to judiciously use cultural skills is key to interpersonal, team, functional and organizational effectiveness.

Appendix A

Guide to Common Culture-Based Challenges

The third column highlights some of the central questions to pursue when conducting cultural due diligence.

Dimension	Common Challenges	
Environment	Empowerment & Role Definition	Do individuals see and/or expect their individual roles as clearly limited and circumscribed? Do they see themselves empowered to take initiatives?
Time	Time Management Problem Solution Work Flow Structure	How driven are individuals by timelines and deadlines? How are timelines and timeframes interpreted?
Action	Relationship Management Trust	How much relationship building and/or team-building is expected? What are the differing expectations for balancing relationship and task management? What are the expectations and needs concerning individual self-disclosure?

Communication	Communication Media Feedback & Conflict Management Rapport Building	Which communication media do individuals prefer and how do they utilize it? How is utilization expected, rewarded and reinforced? How do individuals expect feedback to be provided? What are the norms for each party involved? How directly do individuals expect to address conflict? What is their comfort zone in addressing issues directly/indirectly? What kind of conflict management is expected, reinforced and rewarded? How much emotional alignment is expected in building rapport between parties?
Space	Information Sharing Accountability and Boundaries	Do parties involved share information on a 'need-to-know' or 'good-to-know' basis? To what degree do the parties involved accept shared accountability and authority? How much trust and relationship building is necessary for information to be shared?

Power	Authority & Decision Making	How hierarchical are the decision-making processes within each party? What is expected, reinforced and rewarded? To what degree do individuals expect to operate with clear parameters of authority?
Individualism	Process, Rules & Identity	To what degree are the individuals involved motivated? by group membership or as individual contributors? To what degree do the parties and individuals involved have a sense of uniqueness warranting special consideration and treatment? To what degree do parties and individuals involved expect to implement/follow a common set of rules and procedures?
Competitiveness	Work / Life Balance	To what degree do parties and individuals involved expect to separate work from family and social life? To what degree do the parties and individuals involved allow for a blending of these boundaries? What is expected, reinforced and rewarded concerning the balance between work and the parties involved?

Structure	Role and Process Clarity, Credibility and Trust	How clearly do processes and roles need to be articulated and framed? To what degree do parties involved require leaders to prescribe clear processes and define expectations in order to invest them with credibility and trust?
Thinking	Problem Solving Presentation of Ideas	Do parties and individuals involved focus on the big picture or specific detail? Do parties and individuals involved expect experimentation or abstract reasoning for problem solving? How do parties and individuals involved expect arguments and presentations to be structured? What is the preferred logical flow that is perceived as meaningful?

Appendix B

Definition of Terms

Cultural Continuum
The spectrum between two opposing orientations within a cultural dimension, such as equality-hierarchy or competitive-cooperative.

Cultural Dialogue
The ability to illuminate cultural underpinnings of behavior and performance, close cultural gaps and create cultural synergy through conversation.

Cultural Dimension
An overall category that contains one or more related cultural continua.

Cultural Mentoring
The ability to advise, teach and coach the individuals in one's sphere of influence to (a) recognize the cultural underpinnings and consequences of their behavior, (b) understand the cultural and behavioral requirements for true inclusion, and (c) support change through inclusive behaviors, practices, and approaches (including policies and systems).

Cultural Orientation
A particular culture-based value, such as equality or competitiveness.

Cultural Orientations Approach
A comprehensive, effective and practical method for 1) describing critical value drivers of individual and collective behavior, 2) identifying cultural congruence and gaps using non-judgmental language, and 3) developing appropriate strategies for bridging cultural gaps and creating synergy.

Cultural Orientations Indicator® or COI®
A personal assessment tool that provides individuals with their own cultural profile on the basis of the conceptual framework described by the Cultural Orientations Model™ (COM™).

Cultural Orientations Model™ or COM™
A model of culture introduced in 1995 by Brake, Walker and Walker that combines current concepts of intercultural studies into 10 cultural dimensions, 17 cultural continua and 36 cultural orientations.

Cultural Preference
An overall favoring of a particular cultural orientation, perspective or approach.

Culture
The complex pattern of ideas, emotions and observable manifestations (behaviors and/or symbols) that tend to be expected, reinforced and rewarded by and within a particular group.

Cultural Competence
(1) the ability to reduce the risks and maximize the opportunities inherent in cultural differences and similarities, as well as culture-based performance and success factors.

(2) A key global leadership competency characterized by the ability to convert the awareness of cultural orientation patterns and one's own cultural profile and identity into adaptive behaviors through which to connect with a culturally diverse workforce and customer base.

Culture Gap
The difference in cultural orientations between individuals or between an individual and a social context.

Gap Analysis
The act of contrasting and comparing differences in cultural orientations between individuals or an individual and a social context in order to identify appropriate behavioral strategies for improved communication.

Interaction Analysis
The analysis of interpersonal communication processes in order to gain a better understanding of each party's values, expectations and objectives.

Situation Analysis
The analysis of social contexts in order to gain a better understanding of the meaning, requirements and expectations embedded in social situations.

Social Distance
The level of comfort or discomfort that exists between individuals or groups as a result of differences in cultural orientations.

Style-Switching
The ability to effectively employ a broad and flexible range of behaviors based on an understanding of the cultural orientations pattern of a counterpart or in a given situation in order to attain a desired outcome.

APPENDIX C

Recommended Resources

A suite of web tools and training solution publications have been developed to support the Cultural Orientations Approach to building cultural competence.

1. The Cultural Navigator™

TMC's Cultural Navigator™ is the world's premier technology tool for cultural competence. Using a state-of-the-art web-based platform, the Cultural Navigator™ drives cultural awareness and reduces cultural risk by providing access to a wide range of learning, consulting and assessment solutions in one easy-to-understand, intuitive package. It represents a practical and powerful resource for individuals and clients interested in *improving their global effectiveness*.

The Cultural Navigator™ consists of eight primary channels:

- **Cultural Profile/Cultural Orientations Indicator (COI®)** – the *only statistically validated online self-assessment tool available on the market* assesses individual cultural preferences and allows the user to apply the assessment results to a menu-driven comparative database of countries and regional profiles. Users can compare their personal cultural profiles with those of other cultures and identify areas of commonality as well as areas of cultural differences for which behavioral changes might be considered. Recommendations for behavioral changes are included with each individual profile.

- **CountryScope** – a 100+ country database with a comprehensive cross-cultural comparison of management practices designed to enable users to adapt management styles for improved effectiveness. Recent upgrades to this channel include tabs for *Diversity, Relocation* and *Travel*. CountryScope content is also available for purchase directly through www.CountryScope.com (see below).

- **Learning Zone** – provides access to TMC's blended learning solutions for Global Effectiveness, Leadership and Management Development. TMC's blended learning includes learning labs, virtual classes and coaching in addition to classroom learning, all designed to offer users a customized selection of delivery options to optimize individual learning.

- **Web Learning** – direct access to TMC's flagship *Globalization* and *Cultural Orientations at Work* web courses.

- **Cultural Simulator** - direct access to TMC's proprietary cultural simulations that allow users to test and reinforce awareness and learning by creating on-line simulations around a variety of management topics pertaining to a specific country or region.

- **Exchange Forum/Team Forum** - provides a platform for TMC's growing suite of Cultural Coaching Solutions, as well as creating a community for client users to offer comments and observations that add to the richness of the cultural experience available using the tool. TMC's expert coaches will moderate this feature and provide context and quality assurance.

- **Global Management Toolbox** – a searchable database of InfoPacks™ containing information and tools on global management issues designed to improve cross-cultural management effectiveness.

- **MyNavigator™** is a personal navigation system featuring (i) a user profile to identify the nature of the individual's role and responsibilities, such as business traveler, expatriate, global team leaders, etc., (ii) an individualized navigation dashboard containing pre-selected links that correspond to the user's profile that draws upon the database resources of the Cultural Navigator™ to tailor information based on the user's needs, and (iii) a 'briefing-style' personal report available in print and/or e-mail format.

Visit the Cultural Navigator™ at **www.culturalnavigator.com**.

2. www.CountryScope.com

TMC's newest web offering allows for access to real time, updated information on over 50 countries and regions in all parts of the world. Users can access information as CD-ROMs, downloads or licenses to streaming content.

The information provided is fully integrated with the Cultural Orientations Model and provides a comprehensive introduction to the social and business culture of the specific country and region.

The following countries' information is available on www.countryscope.com:

Argentina, Australia, Austria, Belgium, Brazil, Canada, Chile, China, Colombia, Czech Republic, Denmark, Finland, France, Germany, Hong Kong, Hungary, India, Indonesia, Ireland, Israel, Italy, Japan, Malaysia, Mexico, Netherlands, Norway, Philippines, Poland, Russia, Saudi Arabia, Singapore, South Africa, South Korea, Spain, Sweden, Switzerland, Taiwan, Thailand, Turkey, United Kingdom, United States of America, Venezuela, Vietnam

In addition, the following regions are also available:

Asia/Pacific, Eastern Europe, Western Europe, Middle East and Africa, North America, Latin America

To order, visit www.countryscope.com or www.tmcorp.com.

3. Management Navigator™ - TMC's web tool for management development

The Management Navigator™ is a cutting edge web learning platform designed to help improve leadership and management effectiveness through the targeted identification of learning resources and management topics customized for today's global companies.

Visit www.managementnavigator.com for information about the Management Navigator™.

4. Inclusive Leadership Navigator™

This web-based portal provides users access to a variety of tools to develop or enhance their knowledge and skills as *Inclusive Leaders*. Such tools include:

- Inclusive Leadership Profile (ILP)™
- Information on key Diversity & Inclusion Topics
- Country and region specific *Diversity Profiles*
- *Diversity & Inclusion Simulator*
- *Best Practices and Leadership Tools*

Additional practical tools include:

- **Diversity and Inclusion Audit:** A tool that allows managers to assess their organization's needs with respect to its marketplace, talent (workforce), leadership, and policies and procedures. Contact TMC's Inclusive Leadership practice for details (www.tmcorp.com).

- **Diversity Reports:** Review of workforce and marketplace trends in over twenty countries. Topical reports on global trends.

For detailed information visit www.inclusivenavigator.com.

5. TMC Learning Solutions for Global Effectiveness

TMC's Blended Learning Solutions extend the Cultural Orientations approach to specific domains of management. Each learning solution can be delivered face-to-face, virtually, or developed as a web-delivered program. Each topic is embedded with a thorough cross-cultural perspective and supports managers with global responsibilities:

- Cultural Orientations at Work
- Doing Business Globally
- Managing Across Cultures
- Managing Culture in Global Business
- Multicultural Teamwork
- Leading Global Teams
- Global Project Management
- Negotiating Across Cultures
- Presenting Across Cultures

In addition, country- and region-specific overview workshops are available and can be customized to an organization's learning needs.

To view the TMC Global Effectiveness Curriculum, visit the link http://learningzone.tmcorp.com or www.tmcorp.com and select "Learning Solutions".

Appendix D

Bibliography

Hall, Edward T. *Beyond Culture.* New York, NY: Doubleday, 1981.

Hampden-Turner, C. and Alfons Trompenaars. *The Seven Cultures of Capitalism: Value Systems for Creating Wealth in the United States, Japan, Germany, France, Britain, Sweden and the Netherlands.* New York, NY: Doubleday, 1993.

Harris, Phillip R. and Robert T. Moran. *Managing Cultural Differences.* 3rd Edition. Houston, TX: Gulf Publishing Company, 1991.

Hofstede, Geert. *Culture and Organizations: Software of the Mind.* London, UK: McGraw-Hill, 1991.

Hofstede, Geert. *Culture's Consequences: International Differences in Work-Related Values.* Beverly Hills, CA: Sage, 1980.

Issacs, William. *Dialogue and the Art of Thinking Together.* New York, NY: Doubleday, 1999.

Kluckhohn, F.R. and F.L. Strodtbeck. *Variations in Value Orientations.* Westport, CT: Greenwood Press, 1961.

Kroeber, A. L. and C. Kluckhohn. *Culture: Critical Review of Concepts and Definitions. Vol. 1, No. 1.* Cambridge, MA: Peabody Museum, 1952.

Rhinesmith, Stephen H. *A Manager's Guide to Globalization.* Homewood, IL: Irwin, 1993.

Stewart, Edward C. and Milton J. Bennett. *American Cultural Patterns: A Cross-Cultural Perspective.* Yarmouth, ME: Intercultural Press, 1991.

Stone, Douglas., et al. *Difficult Conversations: How to Discuss what Matters Most.* New York, NY: Penguin Books, 2000.

Trompenaars, Alfons. *Riding the Waves of Culture: Understanding Cultural Diversity in Business.* London: The Economist Books, 1993.

Viney, John. *The Culture Wars: How American and Japanese Businesses Have Outperformed Europe's and Why the Future Will Be Different.* New York, NY: John Wiley & Sons, Inc., 2001.

Walker, Danielle, Thomas Walker and Joerg Schmitz. *Doing Business Internationally.* 2nd Edition. New York, NY: McGraw-Hill, 2000.

Footnotes

[1] This is reflected in the number of definitions researchers have offered to explain it. In 1952, Kroeber and Kluckhohn identified over 150 definitions, most of which describe culture as a pattern of values, beliefs and behaviors that create a sense of identity for a social group and its members.
Many definitions portray culture as a complex, multi-dimensional concept that operates on both a conscious and an unconscious level of individuals and groups. Hofstede (1991) defines it as "the collective programming of the mind that distinguishes members of one human group from another." This perspective emphasizes the cognitive aspect of culture. Edward Hall, in contrast, defines culture as "a system for creating, sending, storing and processing information." He captures both the cognitive and communication aspect of culture. Defined simply as "learned behavior," as others suggest, highlights the behavioral aspects of culture.
Reference: Page 9

[2] **Behavioral Gap:** An individual behaves in a way that directly contrasts with the behaviors and/or expectations of another. For example, a person with a fluid time orientation is consistently late for meetings with a colleague who is fixed-time oriented. The former understands appointment times as approximate, while the latter perceives them as exact. The experience of social distance caused by these differing preferences manifests itself behaviorally in this example. The behavioral manifestation of the **culture gap** may also be experienced cognitively and/or emotionally and may cause frustration and other negative feelings on both sides.
Reference: Page 13

[3] It recognized the research contributions of: Kluckhohn and Strodtbeck, Hall, Hofstede, Hampden-Turner, Trompenaars, Rhinesmith, Stewart and Bennett.
Reference: Page 20

[4] TMC is currently developing a coding system to map the differentiated valuation of cultural orientations across management/business situations. This system will provide a uniform way of decoding behavioral and interaction patterns across cultural environments.
Reference: Page 23

[5] According to Moran and Harris (1991), cultural synergy "builds upon similarities and fuses differences resulting in more effective human activities and systems. The very diversity of people can be utilized to enhance problem solving by combined action."
Reference: Page 127

About the Author

JOERG SCHMITZ serves as Director of Consulting and Learning Solutions at TMC, a global management and leadership consultancy headquartered in Princeton, New Jersey, U.S.A. He initiated and manages the *Cultural Competence, Global Teamwork* and *Inclusive Leadership* practice areas and supervises TMC's research and development activities in these areas.

Mr. Schmitz has designed and implemented consulting and education projects for numerous multinationals, including Schering AG, DaimlerChrysler, Hoffman La Roche, Johnson & Johnson, B/S/H, Pfizer, Citigroup, Corning, American Express, Infosys, Boehringer-Ingelheim, Merck, Merrill Lynch, Air Products and Chemicals, Young & Rubicam, ArvinMeritor and others. He is co-author of *Doing Business Internationally*, 2nd edition (2003, McGraw-Hill) and author of *Transcendent Teams* (2000, Princeton Training Press) and *The Cultural Orientations Guide* (2006, Princeton Training Press).

Mr. Schmitz is a cultural anthropologist trained in communication analysis and educated in his native Germany, Mexico and the United States.